Writing
for Scholarly
Publication

Writing
for Scholarly
Publication

Anne Sigismund Huff

SAGE Publications
International Educational and Professional Publisher
Thousand Oaks   London   New Delhi

For information:

SAGE Publications, Inc.
2455 Teller Road
ThousandOaks, California 91320
E-mail: order@sagepub.com

SAGE Publications Ltd.
6 Bonhill Stree
London EC2A 4PU
United Kingdom

SAGE Publications India Pvt. Ltd.
M-32 Market
Greater Kailash I
New Delhi 110 048 India

Printed in the United States of America

Library of Congress Cataloging-in-Publication Data

Huff, Anne Sigismund.
    Writing for scholarly publication / by Anne Sigismund Huff.
        p. cm.
    Includes bibliographical references (p.).
    ISBN 0-7619-1804-3 (cloth: acid-free paper)
    ISBN 0-7619-1805-1 (pbk.: acid-free paper)
    1. Authorship. 2. Academic writing. 3. Scholarly publishing. I. Title.
    PN146 .H84 1998
    808'.02—ddc21   98-25425

99 00 01 02 03 04 05 10 9 8 7 6 5 4 3 2 1

Acquiring Editor:	Marquita Flemming
Editorial Assistant:	Mary Ann Vail
Production Editor:	Astrid Virding
Production Assistant:	Nevair Kabakian
Typesetter/Designer:	Marion Warren
Cover Designer:	Candice Harman

To
Betsy
&
David
Both excellent writers.

Contents

PART III

Basic Components of Scholarly Writing 65

✣

Preface

I had a very hard time getting something published after receiving my PhD. As with most persistent problems, there were multiple causes, including my rich but unfocused interdisciplinary training, the fact that I had joined a young and disorderly field of study, and an absence of role models for what I was trying to do.

Finally, I realized that my biggest problem was none of these things; I was talking to myself, about issues that reflected idiosyncratic experience and interests, without any clear image of a broader audience. This book summarizes my attempts to move beyond these roadblocks. It is based most of all on the idea that scholarship is a collective endeavor, and writing a central ground for conversation within that collective. Once I realized that I was writing to communicate something to an external audience (obvious perhaps, but I had not kept that idea in mind), my work began to be accepted for publication.

Recognition of the growing pressures on all academics to publish led to a decision to make research and writing for publication a formal part of the doctoral courses I teach. The tone, formal exercises, and shameless advice offered here reflect this context. The students in my courses have a wide range of interests, and most have their own advisers to guide content decisions. In retrospect, these have been helpful constraints; the generic tools I developed are more portable than they would be had I worked within just one discipline. Although my focus is primarily on writing for academic journals, for example, students report that the course has been valuable for working on dissertations. As I've offered faculty workshops, some participants have found help with book-length manuscripts as well.

My aim is to help others orient their work toward publication from the very beginning of a research project. The semester time frame is short, however, and we typically work together with research projects that are nearing completion. I spend a minimum amount of time discussing the writing process. We immediately begin a series of exercises designed to generate two reviewed drafts of an individually written paper that course participants agree to submit to a conference or journal, while they carry out assignments related to the substantive topic of the course as well. Yet almost all papers move far enough to merit external review, and their success rate has been remarkably high.

This book formalizes that set of assignments. You may feel they are too mechanical, and too positivistic. I do. But participants typically praise this aspect of the course. Most like following a specific set of activities aimed at subdividing and demystifying the writing process. Thus I am increasingly confident about my advice, reminding others of Wittgenstein's remark that "after you climb the ladder, you can throw it away."[1]

As with all teaching, I expected to be instructed by this course experience, but I have been surprised by how much I continue to learn. I value my continued work in this area especially because clearer writing is associated with clearer thinking—which is what I wanted to achieve as an academic all along.

I'm glad to conclude by thanking some of those who are thus instructing me. The material in this book has benefited (with the usual disclaimer about remaining shortcomings) from interaction with many people, especially at the University of Illinois, the University of Colorado at Boulder, and Cranfield School of Management. Their support and suggestions have shaped what you will read. Kurt Heppard, in particular, deserves my thanks for bringing a formal manuscript into being through his continuing enthusiasm, his notes from two separate seminars, and help with two appendixes.

I am also indebted to Mary Jo Hatch, who talks about her approach to writing in Appendix A. Jone Pearce discusses the insights that writers from other language traditions bring to the "intellectual café" in Appendix B. Kay Goodman cheerfully prepared more than 150 course overheads, adding humorous and yet highly relevant clip art. (If you would like to use some of these for your own teaching purposes, they can be found on my website—http://spot.colorado.edu/~huff/.) Alexandra

Eikenbary provided invaluable formatting help. Connie Luoto carefully proofed and corrected many "final" drafts. I particularly appreciated her enthusiasm and many suggestions as an early reader. Linda Johanson provided additional helpful comments as an outside reviewer.

My current research and writing is warmly supported by the University of Colorado and the Cranfield Writing Collective. More directly, I benefit from a long collaborative association with Jim Huff that continues to increase the breadth of my endeavors and maintain my interest in scholarship.

Note

1. Wittgenstein, L. (1922). *Tractatus logico-philosphicus* (paperback edition). London: Routledge, p. 189.

Part I

╼❧❧╾

Background

The first two chapters of this book outline the philosophy behind the much more practical chapters that follow. I contend that scholarly writing is conversation—the point I missed when I first tried to publish—but also argue that writing is valuable in itself as a form of scholarly thought. I then urge you, the writer, to actively manage writing and all scholarly activity.

However, if you are eager to get a "quick start" (the option we've grown accustomed to from computer products) turn to Part II.

Chapter 1

⋰⋱

Writing as Conversation

This chapter introduces five basic ideas that recur in the chapters that follow:

- *Scholarly work is rooted in the lively exchange of ideas—conversation at its best.*
- *Written work is the most enduring and often the most influential contribution a scholar makes to academic conversation.*
- *Writing is also important to scholarship because it clarifies thought and thus the generation of new knowledge.*
- *Even procrastinators often begin writing before establishing critical parameters of communication, thus diluting these benefits.*
- *Seeking advice from others, from the beginning, can save time and firmly put writing into a conversational mode.*

Scholarship Is Conversation

Thomas Kuhn helped us see that scholarship requires and is the product of interaction within a scientific community.[1] The content and process of scholarship is learned from other scholars; they shape the way the individual understands the world, and define the issues worth attention. Scholars need this audience to assess and appreciate their work. Even the most iconoclastic individuals are rooted in a social setting.

An important form of interaction among scholars can be usefully defined as *conversation*. The word clearly goes beyond an exchange of information, but I was surprised that the *Oxford English Dictionary* defines it first of all as "the action of living or having one's being in a place or among persons."[2] Conversation is thus the essence of society.

It suggests ongoing dialogue that has the potential not only to add to each participant's store of information but to alter participants' opinions and priorities, even the way they go on to conduct their academic lives. In Appendix B, Jone Pearce suggests that we frequent the same intellectual café.

Let me give you a specific example. About nine months ago, my husband Jim was asked to be the discussant for a keynote speaker at his annual professional meetings. This is the kind of assignment you take seriously. He liked the paper but thought that the author might have missed an alternative explanation for the phenomenon that interested him. This insight was based on previous work that Jim had done in a different subfield, so it was relatively easy to go to the library, get some data, and do some preliminary analysis. This work suggested his hunch was right, and part of his comments about the presentation revolved around this addition. The speaker responded that Jim's line of inquiry would strengthen work in the area, although he remained interested in his major argument. Various members of the audience debated the relative importance of the two lines of attack and suggested a few more of their own. When Jim returned from the meeting, a doctoral student in his department who had been in the audience said she was working in a region that might provide additional insight into Jim's initial arguments. As they talked, they got excited about the possibilities and are now in the process of writing a proposal for government funding. If they get the grant, it will occupy their time for several years. Even if this particular proposal is not funded, Jim's knowledge and current interests have subtly shifted.

Academic conversations are often like this. They take place over time, draw in people from different institutions, at different points in their academic careers. They move from individual to joint work, from private to public settings. Any one conversation won't affect all participants' work—but our endeavors are indelibly shaped by ongoing interactions among colleagues.

It is impossible to anticipate this flow of influence. Surely you have been delighted by a conversation with someone you did not anticipate would be so interesting, and surprised by the impact of "exactly the right word at the right time." Scholarship is like that, and newcomers are an important source of its vitality. Conversation occurs in the classroom, among colleagues at the same institution, at conferences, by e-mail. It occurs most of all via the written word. At least at the present time, journals, books, and their electronic substitutes are the basic means by which the scholarly community carries out its work. These written words are not just the repository of past and current findings. Through the subject matter covered, the methods used, the reviews written, the arguments and agreements presented, writing in journals and other outlets defines a field and shapes its future.

To share your ideas and fully participate in the scholarship of your field, you therefore must *write*. This is the first reason to pay attention to writing. Writing is not just a way of communicating conclusions from your scholarly endeavors, it is a more basic means of participating in scholarship itself. Our efforts to communicate, especially within the disciplining confines of the written word, help us develop an intrinsic understanding of the tacit norms and subtle nuances that characterize good scholarship.

It is important to recognize that many different conversations are taking place at the same time, even in relatively small fields. Each scholarly subfield understands the world in a somewhat different way and focuses on somewhat different issues. Some fields have a long tradition, with many accepted assumptions; others are still sorting out the basic rules of the game. These complexities merely underscore the importance of being an active participant in the field and having a knowledge of scholarly conversation that is rich and current. The more intricate the conversation, the more you need to clarify your ideas in writing and submit them to others for further refinement. The more the boundaries of a field are unclear, and the need for and nature of the work to be done is the subject of debate, the more you need to test your ideas in writing and submit them to others for their response.

Of course, "the scholarly community" is not always accessible. And it may not always be right. So individuals need to develop their own sense of the world and what new knowledge is worth having. Stories about influential scholarship often involve individual perseverance when other scholars did not recognize the significance of the work being pursued. But the "internal compass" directing our scholarship should not blind us to the importance of seeking out and connecting with a larger community interested in similar issues. Good scholarship, that is rigorous and tested and useful to others, results from interaction within such a community.

Before you begin to write, I therefore suggest you focus on your own scholarly community.

EXERCISE 1

*Identify the people, topics, and specific works that
provide the intellectual foundation of your project.*

I have in mind a rather personal account, but one that other members of your scholarly community would recognize. The format might take the form of a family tree, but you can make connections visible in any way you like. Your overview should have a temporal dimension; think of work that excites you, look at the key bibliographic works those authors cite, perhaps go further back into the bibliographies of these works. Include significant works written by specific individuals. You should be able to show multiple influences on your work and may find that geographic centers of past accomplishments are of interest. The objective is to establish your location in the social space of scholarship as a first step toward becoming more actively involved.

Good Thinking and Good Writing
Are Intrinsically Linked

One of Karl Weick's famous aphorisms is, "How can I know what I think until I see what I say?"[3] Initially enigmatic to many, this question is more easily accepted as a reminder that experience often precedes cognition.

But I suggest that the relationship is a circular one. Another side of Karl's equation is, "How can I improve what I write until I find out what I think?" In other words, we write to think better, and as we think better we write better, as shown in Figure 1.1.

Taking this point of view adds another dimension to the idea that writing is at the heart of scholarly activity. We do not write just to compete in the "publish or perish" game. Writing *is* the game because

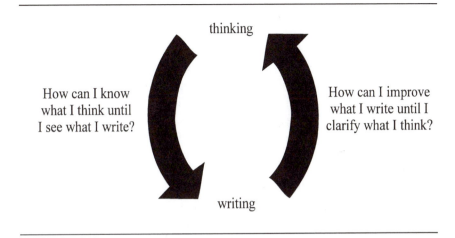

thinking

How can I know
what I think until
I see what I write?

How can I improve
what I write until I
clarify what I think?

writing

Figure 1.1. The Reciprocal Relationship of Writing and Thinking

it almost inevitably improves thinking about what questions to ask, and how to answer those questions. As I have worked to improve my writing, I am confident that my capacity to think through complicated issues, design more innovative and important research, and carry it through have also improved. My ideas are rarely well articulated until they are written down. More precisely, they are rarely well articulated until they are *re*written, subjected to detailed conversation with others, and rewritten again.

The first critical step in this process of needed improvement is to open a new computer file and begin putting words in a row. As I begin to write, I realize that the A-B-C-D progression of ideas that seemed so obvious in the night, in the car driving to work, in my mind as I read the literature, or even as I delivered the lecture, is not that simple. There are always mental gaps that have to be filled and sequences that must be reordered. Once I begin to write, I realize that I cannot convincingly make C follow B; I need to reorganize my thinking. Further, it often becomes obvious that D is not the logical conclusion. It needs to be followed by other ideas, which I have not yet developed. In grappling with the organization of ideas, I usually realize that I must make hard choices about purpose, audience, and outlet. I must clarify my intended contribution, especially to myself. The precision that can be found in writing thus is critical from the very beginning of the scholarly process.

In Parts I and II of this book, I will talk about choices that apply to *both* research and writing. At the beginning of a scholarly project, writing can streamline research design and add elegance to analysis. Similar benefits can be gained when starting to write about a project that is essentially completed. When you are just starting a scholarly project, I encourage you to go through the first exercises in this book, even though I generally use them with people who arrive in a course with their research design, data collection, and analysis substantially completed. There are different ways to describe any project, and different audiences will be interested in hearing about different aspects of what you have done. These introductory chapters are written in the firm belief that it is better to explicate the framework for what you will write before you begin. It is very painful to be told after months of research and writing effort that the audience for your work is not obvious, that too many subjects are being considered, and that the contribution of the work is not clear. Chapter 3 considers these issues in more detail.

Deciding *When* to Begin Writing Is Critical

If you begin writing too soon, your thinking may be so embryonic that you do not find the effort very clarifying. If you wait too long to write, you are likely to have so many ideas they are difficult to organize and express clearly. Of course, the right time to begin depends upon your thinking and working habits, but in my experience most of us get into a double bind: We wait too long to begin but then waste time writing because we still have not made important decisions about the basic components of successful communication.

A strong organizing thread in this book thus is as follows:

❧   ☙

Think before you write.
Then, write to help you rethink.

❧☙❧☙

The critical questions to answer are these:

- Which conversations should I participate in?
- Who are the important "conversants"?
- What are these scholars talking about now?
- What are the most interesting things I can add to the conversation?

These are not easy questions. Typically, scholars are aware of and interested in more than one subgroup and quite a few conversations. At this point you must consider the literature in your field. Survey the many scholarly conversations that have been taking place over the last few years and identify those that seem most interesting and important to you. Also focus on conversations that you feel will continue for some time. Scholarship is subject to fads, and conversations run their course. To find conversations that are likely to continue long enough for you to make a contribution, pay more attention to what is being written and discussed at meetings, in working papers, and in electronic exchanges than in journals and books.

My advice is to find a few conversations and actively imagine yourself "talking back" to your colleagues from the very beginning of your career. As you define specific interests and conversations, begin to write. Even though you may not see your ideas in print for some time, the exercise will improve your thinking, your research, and thus your chances for ultimate publication.

Let me be very clear about the reason I am urging you to do all this work:

❧ ❧

You should anticipate making an impact on the scholarly conversation of your field, from the very beginning of your career.

❧❧

By suggesting that you pay more attention to scholarly conversation, I am encouraging you to make a worthwhile contribution to that conversation. Sometimes authors are too hesitant. They think they will have to wait until they have more experience before joining the conversations that interest them most. Don't be that tentative. Begin by thinking in terms of the people and the ideas that interest you most. Assertive, well-grounded responses to those who have captured your interest are rewarding and fun to make. These responses are the best representatives of the time you are investing in your scholarly career. They are the most likely to be published, and cited by others.

Thinking, Writing, and Contribution
Are Improved by Seeking Advice

You don't have to isolate yourself in your early steps toward ultimate publication, although far too many of us do. It seems obvious to me that I do my best thinking (and writing) when interacting with others. Why then do I wait so long to seek advice about the things I am writing? A major reason is that I'm reluctant to ask others to waste time on ideas that I myself know are still only partially formed. Another reason is that I am respectful of my colleagues' time.

But, basically, I'm afraid—afraid they will think that I'm not as smart as I want them to think I am, afraid that my emerging ideas could be jinxed by premature exposure to others, afraid these ideas are not as worthy as I hope they are.

I also do not *give* advice as often as I might. Here again, I am hesitant. I don't want to squelch my colleagues or their ideas. I am respectful of their efforts. But the major reason that I don't offer advice more often is that I don't have enough time. Many things impinge upon my writing; working on other people's writing keeps me away from what I want to do most, *my* writing.

Both dynamics stymie scholarly conversation, and thus the progress of scholarship. The desirable solution is easy to state but hard to do. First, get tough. People hesitate to seek or give advice because they do not sufficiently separate ideas from their carriers. But what I am thinking about today is a very small part of who I am, and what you are thinking about today says relatively little about who you are. When we have our most noble thoughts about scholarly inquiry, we say we are engaged in a joint endeavor to understand the world. That is a good image to bring down to the everyday world of writing. Remember that we have a common commitment to expand understanding.

Second, minimize the burden. The chapters that follow are based on the confidence that the benefits of seeking advice far exceed the pain. The benefit received can be vastly increased if you follow this prescription:

⁙ ⁙

Ask for help often, but keep requests to read an
entire manuscript to a minimum.

⁙⁙

It is relatively easy, and much less painful, to get a response to a title, abstract, outline, even introduction, than to an entire manuscript. Another advantage of focusing on these specific parts of scholarly writing is that their established function may lead to more explicit advice. Putting forth parts of a manuscript also makes it possible to move into the advice-getting mode much earlier in the writing process. You will be thinking in terms of conversation from the very beginning— testing and improving your ability to clearly say something of interest to others.

Community Is Important and Must Be Nurtured

Your chances of getting advice will increase significantly if you can establish a continuing connection with a small set of people who will converse about your field of inquiry (even though they may not be part of it) and make an ongoing effort to read your attempts to participate in that community. As a second preparatory step to working with this book, I therefore encourage you to name fellow travelers who are or might be involved in the process of improving both your thinking and your writing.

EXERCISE 2

Identify potential members of your "writing community."

I have used this as an early exercise in a number of workshops on writing and have been amazed at the variety of answers people provide. Peers interested in the same subfield typically are just the beginning of a long list that might include more senior colleagues, noted figures in the field, people in other fields, spouses, partners, parents, personal friends, and acquaintances who are not at all interested in the specific subject of study.

Reading such lists leads me to several general observations. First, everyone has contacts who might be helpful for improving their writing. Second, we need different kinds of readers at different points in the scholarly process. Third, it makes sense to be explicitly strategic about asking for advice. Fourth, we can learn from those whose motives are suspect, but these learning possibilities are unlikely to be the basis for an ongoing advice-giving relationship.

I believe the most sustaining sources of advice are found within a group that has a history and a commitment to the future. In this community, trust is desirable; it greatly broadens the scope of conversation if few topics are off limits. Honesty (leavened with care) then deepens the content of the exchange; again, the issue is maximizing the scope of what can be said.

Even when you are part of such a community, it pays to think about how you will interact with it. Some people are likely to give more caring and supportive feedback than others; some people (including some of the caring ones) are likely to be more honest than others. Early contact may provide "shaping" insight, while later contact could elicit more specific and tailored feedback. Sometimes I seek out people I can count on to be enthusiastic because they too love the questions that interest me, because they love me, or because they are blessed by a sunny disposition in general. At other times, it may be more efficient to hear an opposing point of view—if I can preserve the essential parts of my work with a strong internal compass. I'm also going to consider whether it makes sense to reserve the input of a senior colleague who could affect my career for critiquing the things that I've already fine-tuned with the advice of others. In short, it makes sense to establish ongoing high-trust relationships, which is why I invite you to work on another exercise.

EXERCISE 3

Think of at least three things you can do to form and then sustain your writing community.

If you took some time with this exercise, you probably identified quite a variety of things that can be done to support community, from establishing a formal time for conversation to going bowling. What works to form and maintain a group is as varied as groups are varied; the key is to think innovatively about ways to maintain commitment. Reciprocity appears to be critical. If you are lucky, you will occasionally be able to ask your adviser, your spouse, or others in unique relationships to lend you a helping hand with your writing. A more reliable source of help can be had when both parties' writing benefits from the advice-giving process—in my experience, that means individuals who each believe they will genuinely benefit from the advice of the other. Often, but not always, they are at roughly the same level of experience and ability.

Good Advice Takes Care

Whether the request is long or short, it is helpful to know what would be most useful to say as a reviewer in an advice-giving relationship. At the end of this book in Appendix C, Kurt Heppard offers a checklist. It's a good list for those who are asked to provide formal reviews for journals, grant proposals, and other outlets. It is equally useful as a guideline for responding to members of your own writing community when they ask for your advice about the content of what they are writing. The following more general observations about advice-giving also may be helpful:

1. *Make sure you know what the writer wants to accomplish.* Nothing stymies conversation more quickly than misinterpreting your colleague's intentions.

2. *Identify positive aspects of the current manuscript.* We learn at least as much from other people's opinion about what we do well as from their opinion about what we should change. Furthermore, positive reinforcement lays a very strong foundation for hearing subsequent suggestions for improvement.

3. *Organize and prioritize your ideas about needed change.* Reviewing another person's writing is hard work, but the work is likely to have much greater impact if you take a bit more time to consolidate and prioritize your observations. More specifically, flag the two or three actions that you think would *most* improve what you have read.

4. *Make sure you are not imposing your agenda on their work.* Even two individuals who share the same interests, have similar training, and are trying to talk within the same scholarly community will not write in the same way. It's a point worth remembering as a reviewer. The most helpful advice is not what *you* would do but what you think the *author* should do.

5. *Don't hoard your insights.* In the process of responding to the work that comes your way for comment, there is sometimes a little black voice that whispers, "Don't give away your best ideas!" My advice is to ignore that insidious voice. Ideas are cheap—making something of them is difficult. Ideas that are not exercised in the public arena are less likely to grow and make room for new and improved insights.

Once in a while I recognize an idea of "mine" that someone else has adopted without credit; typically, they don't even remember the source. So be it. Community is not possible for people who are hypersensitive about their own possessions. Furthermore, the way another person develops "my" idea makes it quickly theirs rather than mine. Often I wouldn't have made anything of it anyway, but if I want to pursue the idea further, I can in turn build on the work they have accomplished. If the exchange of ideas does not seem to be mutually beneficial, I don't have to include Benedict Arnold in further conversation. But I have found that this is rarely necessary. In very rare circumstances, it may be smart to keep an insight "off the street" until you have developed it. In general, I believe that you are unlikely to develop such an idea to its full potential if you are paranoid about ownership. Good science is built through good conversation. Good conversation has few boundaries.

6. Be supportive; this is hard work! Although it is true that some people need favorable feedback more than others, I am amazed at how supportive words positively influence almost everyone. Research and writing are essentially lonely activities. We are required to define an agenda that will make a unique contribution to scholarship. There may not be many people working on the issues we choose. However many there are, we quickly become more expert on "our" subject than almost anyone we know. Positive interaction transcends loneliness and is very important. It builds trust—trust that allows members of a community to challenge each other with vigor, giving and receiving hard, honest feedback.

7. Reflect back on your own work. I have found that improving my ability to give advice has meant I give myself better advice as well, but the benefits of reviewing will not be gained by either party without effort. It is very easy for authors to move away from a painful exchange with too little learned. Quick distancing is even more likely for reviewers. To increase the rewards of reviewing, I suggest that one of the rules of your writing community should be that reviewers consider the ideas they offer in the context of their own interests. I have found that what starts as an effort to be supportive often ends by intellectually engaging me, potentially generating the kind of scholarly conversation we all seek.

8. Develop and maintain an internal compass. You do have to be careful when seeking and giving advice, especially if you do it early and often as I advise. An inept remark can easily derail an author from a worthy project. Advice from a group is often contradictory. Suggestions for change may not be on target; after all, they are of necessity based on much less time thinking about your project than you have invested. Perhaps most insidious, in my experience, bad habits are contagious.

As a reviewer, it is worth worrying about what might seep back into your own work.

Conclusion

Academic writing has its own rules and its own creativity. It is also like all other kinds of writing, and you therefore may benefit from the many books available to those who write in other genres. The bibliography summarizes a few of the many sources available.

I find it remarkably easy to identify with these books. Alongside our writing brethren, we choose our subject, try to develop content that will engage others, and work in relative isolation with vacillating confidence in our ultimate success. If writing is hard, perhaps it is because it forces us to "go public" with the inescapable responsibility of these choices. But if we do not engage in conversation, we ultimately have to give up the idea that we are scholars.

Annie Dillard describes writing as wrestling with alligators in her book *The Writing Life*.[4] She once saw a real alligator win a contest with a man in the Everglades. Various studies indicate that the average academic paper is cited only a very few times by other scholars over the many years that follow publication. The more we think seriously about good conversation as the basis of scholarship, and learn to be better conversants, the more we can beat these dismal odds. The alligators should not win!

Notes

1. Kuhn, T. (1970). *The structure of scientific revolutions* (2nd ed.). Chicago: University of Chicago Press.

2. *The compact edition of the Oxford English dictionary.* (1971). Oxford: Oxford University Press.

3. Weick, K. (1995). *Sensemaking in organizations*. Thousand Oaks, CA: Sage, pp. 12, 18.

4. Dillard, A. (1990). *The writing life*. New York: Harper, p. 75.

Chapter 2

÷§÷

Managing Scholarship

Writing interacts with other scholarly activities to change a project's scope and focus. This chapter discusses the utility of deliberately:

- *Expanding understanding by exploring alternative paths of inquiry*
- *Cutting away alternatives to regain the concentration necessary to make a specific contribution*
- *Using joint authorship to expand/contract project definition*
- *Managing time and other writing inputs*

Scholarly Activities Tend to Follow a "Crooked Accordion Path" of Expansion and Contraction

Scholarship can have many aims, but all of them involve doing something that has not been done before. Even the scholar who replicates a study, or codifies previous work, aims to make a new contribution to understanding. This is not easy work. Typically, I start with an idea of what I want to accomplish and begin on one or more scholarly tasks—a literature review, an experiment, discussion with others, or possibly a very rough draft. Almost any task, especially at the beginning of a project, is likely to change the definition of interest considerably, either broadening or narrowing the idea I started with. A literature review, for example, will almost certainly suggest new ideas and variables as well as interesting models and propositions that haven't been considered.

Alternatively, looking at the literature can narrow the initial definition of a project by highlighting how much work has already been done.

The process of expanding and then contracting project scope tends to reiterate itself several times, with this interesting characteristic: refocusing typically emphasizes somewhat different aspects of a project. Similarly, a new expansion usually has a different purpose than the one that preceded it, as shown in Figure 2.1.

The excitement of scholarship often comes from the twists and turns of this "accordion path." I rarely feel in control of the process, but I know the two engines of the accordion process: brainstorming and decision making.

At some points I know that I need more inputs to my research or writing. To expand my current focus, I must be open to new ideas. As I search, many things are likely to seem relevant. I may generate more data or discover new sources in the literature. Conversations with others, browsing the web—almost any activity can broaden my understanding. Even subjects that seem far from my topic can have relevant content. This is a brainstorming mode, which means concentrating on collection and not paying too much attention to evaluation. I know my purpose, but I try not to overdefine it because I expect to discover a more compelling purpose. In the process, there is often a wonderful interaction between various aspects of the project, so that the discovery of a new idea, or instrument or whatever, will redefine other parts of the overall endeavor, like dropping a stone in a pool.

But sooner or later I am overwhelmed by the turbulence I've created. I've collected too many ideas to work with; I've become interested in too many conversations. Interactions among data and ideas have become more confusing than enlightening. It is time to make some decisions. The word *decision* has the perfect etymology for the task. The "*ci*" root means "to cut," which makes "de*ci*sion" a cousin of *scissor* and *incisor*. Cutting back is exactly what must happen if I am to make progress when I am writing. I have to select the most interesting ideas, identify one or two conversations to listen to, commit to one central thesis or message. This often means commitment to specific aspects of a few conversations, as shown in Figure 2.2.

As the project continues, the swings I experience are not so uncontrolled but often involve dramatic turns. I may decide, for example, to join the contents of what I initially thought would be two different

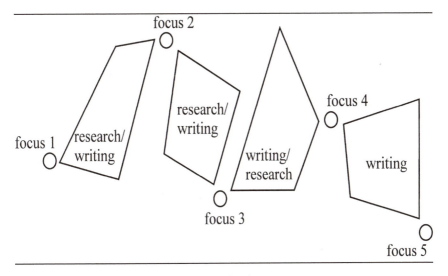

Figure 2.1. The Accordion Path of Scholarship

papers. I may abandon a subject that I first thought would be a central part of my contribution.

I first experienced these disconcerting shifts when writing my dissertation. I felt as if I were on a roller coaster. Often, writing still feels like that, but now at least I feel I have more control over the ride. In fact, charting the course is part of the excitement.

Stand close to your work; examine it in detail. Then stand back, think about its place in the general field, consider its relationship to other areas of inquiry. You are likely to find that both of these activities change the scope and the focus of your endeavor. In general, any change in perspective is likely to have an impact. Consider your work from an unfamiliar theoretic perspective; think about how you would describe it to your mother. But, be careful. I try to work within a framework until I really need a new perspective. I don't want to be whipsawed unnecessarily.

The nature of your scholarly path will depend upon the conversation to be joined, the contribution you envision, and your intellectual proclivities. However, understanding where you have been and where you want to go can save time in subsequent management of the project—thus another exercise.

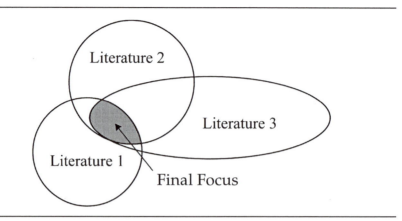

Figure 2.2. Finding the Focus of Your Writing Project

EXERCISE 4

Summarize the history and anticipated future of one of your most recent writing projects by charting its "accordion path."

You may not have a specific writing project in mind to work on next. In Chapter 3, I will urge you to commit to one project, because I think the only way to improve writing is to reflect upon the actual experience of writing. Chapter 3 also has more specific advice about brainstorming and decision making. In the meantime, you may discover something about the path of scholarship, and perhaps your own strengths and weaknesses in managing the process, if you summarize the accordion path of the *last* research or writing project you worked on.

Joint Authorship Can Be a Help or a Hindrance

Scientific inquiry is moving toward more joint projects in almost all fields, with more varied, often international collaboration. The advantages of seeking partners in a research/writing project are many. In many cases, the sheer scope of large projects requires more than one person's effort.

Of particular relevance to the preceding discussion, working with others can help broaden or narrow your research and writing efforts. Coauthors can increase the scope of what you might undertake because of their different training, experience, and insight. They can provide depth by adding issues that you are not as likely to consider. Together you may thus make a greater contribution to the conversation you are joining than any one of you could alone.

If you decide to involve others in your project, there also are the advantages of *camaraderie* (defined in the dictionary on my desk as "familiar, buoyant spirit proper to good comrades, characterized especially by mutual trust and loyalty"[1]). Commitment to such companions can carry you through the dark days that might otherwise cause you to abandon a project, and can even revive a moribund project. Alternatively, a coauthor can help make the necessary decision to abandon an ill-conceived project.

Coauthorship is especially tempting because it seems that sharing the load will allow you to participate in more research and writing projects than you could carry out alone. Although this is certainly true, collaboration takes time. Furthermore, in my experience it is easy to overcommit. Many jointly conceived projects are never published because they die at the back of a coauthor's crowded desk.

An even more unhappy possibility is that the project dies of irreconcilable differences, with residual bitterness among colleagues who would otherwise happily continue to converse. You have much more control as a single author and can efficiently use your time and energy to bring an interesting project to conclusion.

Perhaps the most important pitfall of joint authorship has to do with its potential impact on your reputation in the field of inquiry that interests you. If your name is connected with certain subjects, if you are known to have expertise, and are linked with contributions that attract attention, you are likely to be asked to join other conversations. You will be invited to speak, to join symposia, to contribute to edited books, or to write a book of your own. These are the rewards of scholarship, and they will expand your abilities. The risk of jointly written work is that it may contribute less to your scholarship and reputation.

I advise only that you be purposeful and that you think about the utility of committing to some single-authored work. Specific contributions to a jointly written article or book are rarely clear. The project that falls within the joint abilities of two or more authors is less likely to represent the core agenda of any one. Shared tasks mean that some authors do not have the opportunity to develop skills that will be useful in subsequent projects.

When you do become involved in joint projects, I can suggest three rules that have made a real difference in my work. They emerged from a project I did with Michael Moch.

1. Commit to fast turnaround. Mike and I fell into a turnaround contest when we first started working together. Sometimes a draft was returned within an hour or two! It was fun. We were continuously aware of what the other was trying to accomplish. As our enthusiasm grew, we became even more committed to fast response, and the paper was completed more quickly than any other paper I have written.

2. Assume "ownership" of the paper while it is on your desk. Coauthors, especially in new relationships, often feel compelled to be polite. They may not like (or understand) the material just added by their coauthor, but they feel that the tacit rules of the game are to work around the other person's contribution. Mike and I made the opposite rule explicit. We agreed that nothing was sacred. We freely revised each other's material.

3. Don't revive old text. If the next draft came back with some cherished input missing, we agreed that it was against the rules to cut and paste from the last draft. We could put the idea we wanted to express back into the paper, but it had to be rewritten. As a result of always treating the paper as our own, we both ended up "owning" it, and it was more smoothly written than many coauthored papers where individual voices are still apparent.

Once I experienced how much fun it was to work under these rules, I have suggested them to all subsequent coauthors. They continue to impress me as highly productive rules that get around some major difficulties of coauthorship. They are especially important if there is a status or experience difference among authors.

Self-Management Is Required

I have been talking about "self-management" throughout this chapter. I emphasize it because I realized in another helpful flash of insight (unfortunately, once again long after I began trying to publish) that I had unconsciously decided it wasn't appropriate to manage writing. I think my sherry-sipping view of intellectual life got in the way.

The problem is that the managed parts of life (teaching schedules, committee assignments, even monthly Cub Scout meetings) easily drive out the unmanaged. To get writing done, I had to organize, which began with an inventory of my current practices. I encourage you to do the same. Remember, time spent organizing before writing begins will save time later on.

EXERCISE 5

Identify the times, places, and conditions that most facilitate your writing.

EXERCISE 6

Identify strategies for protecting and enhancing your best writing times.

The basic conclusions I have come to from these exercises are that actually getting sustained writing done takes active management on my part, and that habits and routines are more powerful than good intentions and serendipity. More explicitly, I've found the following management steps very useful:

- Specifying and ordering the *tasks* that must be accomplished to carry out a project
- Deliberately selecting the *time* and *place* for tasks to be done
- Establishing *systems* for controlling material (a filing system, computer backup, and so on)
- *Investing* in needed equipment and assistance (a good printer at home because I often work at home, hiring someone to input data if I have collected a lot, and so on)
- Providing *enriching inputs* (conferences, journal scanning, field trips, and so on)
- *Monitoring* successful performance by others, and deliberately seeking *advice* from those who are already skilled at the work I want to do
- *Learning* from my own attempts to do research and write about it
- *Routinizing* the practices that work well for me

I suggest that you think of yourself as a hired consultant. Ask what you would advise someone in your situation. Good management is often very obvious; we just do not take the time for it. Far more time is lost because we try to work without this oversight.

Conclusion

Virginia Woolf has an interesting description of scholarly work in *To the Lighthouse:*

> For if thought is like the keyboard of a piano, divided into so many notes, or like the alphabet is ranged in twenty-six letters all in order, then [Professor Ramsay's] splendid mind had no sort of difficulty in running over those letters one by one, firmly and accurately, until it had reached, say, the letter Q. He reached Q. Very few people in the whole of England ever reached Q. . . . But after Q? What comes next? After Q there are a number of letters the last of which is scarcely visible to mortal eyes, but glimmers red in the distance. Z is only reached once by one man in a generation. Still if he could reach R it would be something. Here at least was Q. . . .
>
> R is then—what is R? . . . In a flash of darkness he heard people saying—he was a failure—that R was beyond him. He would never reach R.[2]

This description evocatively captures the desperation we all sometimes feel as scholars. At the same time, it didn't seem quite right to me when

I first read it in school; I was sure that scholarly thought was not so linear.

Now I have a clearer sense that it is our job to create orderly arguments precisely because thought *is* unruly. But I continue to doubt the necessity of running against one unyielding roadblock. When stymied by the contribution beyond Q, the scholar should not just pace up and down the veranda as Professor Ramsay did, or stare at the computer screen in increasing frustration. We have to find the judo hold that allows us to rearrange the alphabet or contribute to some other line of inquiry. Harder thinking and better writing are important ingredients in that process, but not the only ones. As scholars we can (and must) try to manage what is happening. We can choose other scholarly activities—reading, teaching, collecting data, and most of all talking with others—that will narrow or broaden the focus of inquiry.

The judo metaphor emphasizes that we must always try to leverage our assets—to use the "weight" we have to best advantage. A proactive stance makes it possible to get beyond the blocks we all experience in scholarship. That is important. More than any other objective, I am writing this book in the hope it will leave readers with more enthusiasm and more commitment to making a contribution through writing. Please keep this thought in mind:

⁌ ⁋

Although writing is time-consuming and difficult,
you should anticipate getting better at it and
discovering more pleasure in it.

⁌⁋⁌⁋

Notes

1. *The new lexicon Webster's encyclopedic dictionary of the English language* (Canadian edition). (1988). New York: Lexicon.
2. Woolf, V. (1927). *To the lighthouse.* New York: Harcourt, Brace & World, pp. 54-55.

Part II

❦

Before Writing Begins:
Choices That Make
Publication More Likely

Since you are reading a book about writing, you have
already made a commitment to think about what you are
trying to do. In this part of the book, I urge you to outline
your writing alternatives, and decide how they fit in a
broader portfolio, so that you can more confidently devote
yourself to the one paper you are going to work on now.
Then, I suggest that you identify a small set of articles (or
books) as the "recipients" of your contribution to scholarly
conversation, while also finding examples of work with
similar objectives to help you make stylistic decisions once
you begin to write.

Chapter 3

※

Choosing a Topic

It is not easy to find a topic that will maintain your interest over the full time period required to advance understanding. Then, too, many people write papers of personal interest that attract little enthusiasm from others. Two activities increase the probability that your topic is both personally absorbing and connects with an audience:

- *brainstorming techniques that increase the variety of topics to choose among,*
- *then juxtaposing your interests, the interests of others in the field, the demands of the subject, and your other commitments to decide among writing alternatives.*

Brainstorming Generates Alternatives From Which More Informed Choices Can Be Made

Many people do not seriously consider their alternatives before beginning a research or writing project. Although it is possible to become frozen in the headlights of too many choices, I think that it is well worth the time to generate and analyze alternatives before beginning work.

In fact, purposeful choice is *the* most important thing you can do to increase scholarly productivity and impact, although luck plays a part that cannot be anticipated, and intuitive leaps are to be valued. Unfortunately, planning is not emphasized in most graduate schools or in most conversations among scholars. Rather than planning, many scholars focus on the interesting intricacies of the tasks at hand. I tend to plan less than I think I should, but when I do pause to reflect, I almost always think the break was worthwhile.

The bibliography lists a few books on brainstorming techniques that are well worth reading as a first critical step in more purposeful thinking about alternatives. I hope you are familiar with the basic rules; nonetheless, they are worth repeating.

1. *Autonomous idea generation without evaluation.* As you begin brainstorming, it is important to delineate your own ideas so that other sources do not overly determine the parameters of your thinking. You should move away from the literature describing previous work, and what well-known scholars in your field think should be done next, to give your own inherent creativity space to "play" with research and later writing alternatives. By extension, move away from what your adviser, your smartest colleagues, and other influential people in your life think. In fact, do not think about what *you* think. The cardinal rule of brainstorming is to generate ideas first, without evaluation.

2. *Varied inputs from other sources.* After you have sketched out quite a few alternatives for a research project or specific piece of writing, add the insights of others. Brainstorming activities are designed to generate a wider pool of ideas than you would normally create. One of the most reliable means of doing so is to interact with others—ideally in face-to-face fanciful conversation, although interaction with written materials can also be generative. Obviously, the more you expose yourself to sources you do not normally encounter, or find modes of conversation that are out of the ordinary, the more novelty is likely, and novelty is what you are seeking.

3. *Playful curiosity and development.* Once you have a pool of ideas, see what happens when you juxtapose, combine, and extend them. The objective is to generate a lot of alternatives to work with, including some "off-track" material that may provide an interesting twist that will increase your contribution to the field.

4. *Delayed evaluation.* Suppressing judgment includes censoring the internal doubts and external comments that inhibit pursuing a

train of thought into new territory. Having fun and being playful are the desired modes of behavior. Yet, ultimately, choices are made. Brainstorming ends as you specify criteria for evaluation and choose among the rich set of alternatives that have been developed. The outcome of this deliberate process of stretch and collapse has been shown to be very productive for some serious and profitable activities, such as new product development and the solution of vexing scientific problems.

Break the Task Into Components, Brainstorm on Each Component

A useful technique for increasing your pool of novel ideas is to break a subject of inquiry into its attributes. For an example adapted from Koberg and Bagnall,[1] consider Figure 3.1 as the first output of a conversation (with oneself or with others) on "designing a new writing instrument."

With such a list, you can easily construct a whole range of new objects to write with. You could design, for example, a square paper box filled with beet juice. That first idea might not make it to the store shelves, but you have quickly freed yourself of preconceptions about ballpoints and graphite pencils. And I can imagine that some potentially marketable ideas might ultimately come out of fanciful speculation about who might be interested in a square paper beet juice pen and how they might use it.

It's easy to anticipate what I'm going to suggest you do next. In my view, few scholars take enough time to think about the almost infinite range of opportunities for carrying out research before they commit themselves to one project. When it is time to write about a project, they similarly do not explore the wide range of alternatives available. Even when they pause to reflect, few are as creative as they might be.

I believe that the richer the "gene pool" of ideas, the more interesting, more varied, and more useful the products of scholarship are likely to be. Therefore I recommend that you think for a few moments about Exercise 7. It will probably be more illuminating if you can get one or two colleagues to do the same thing independently.

Size	Shape	Color	Material	Marker
small	cylinder	black	wood	graphite
medium	sphere	blue	plastic	ink
large	box	rainbow	paper	beet juice
	oval	marbled		

Figure 3.1. Design Alternatives for a Writing Instrument .
Based on Koberg and Bagnall (1976).

EXERCISE 7

Identify basic categories and alternatives within categories that could be used to define your scholarly work.

There are obviously many different approaches to this assignment. If other people thought about the same exercise, you should have more dimensions than you personally identified, even if you thought you were being quite creative. Figure 3.2 suggests an initial list that can be easily changed or elaborated. (You might note that I deliberately did not try to make the alternatives mutually exclusive.)

You could go on to outline the many different paradigms that inform research and writing, from a logical-positivist perspective to postmodernism and beyond. Then, think about the various fields that could inform the kind of work you do, from economics to anthropology to neurology. Follow that list by outlining, in a few areas, the various theories that interest you. Move on to methodological alternatives. (I

Audience	Format	Purpose	Approach
Close Peers	Formal Paper	Inform	Extend Theory
Another Field	Presentation	Persuade	Present Data
International	Essay	Describe	Review Literature
Academic		Explore	
Practitioner			

Figure 3.2. Writing Alternatives

am following a quite structured view of scholarly choices here, as shown in Figure 3.3.)

By playing with permutations from Figures 3.2 and 3.3, it is possible to generate a large number of "beet juice" alternatives that are unlikely to lead to viable scholarly activities. But finding different ways of thinking about scholarly endeavors is an important early task to ensure that you are making an informed choice about your writing alternatives.

Identifying Your Paper Alternatives

All this has been merely a "warm-up" for the beginning of the real work. Now you have to consider your own research and training, your own interests, ambitions, and resources, and come up with specific alternatives for your next project. When I ask my students to do this task (even first-year PhD students), I suggest that they set as a goal generating *at least* one writing project a day for a week. They have courses, the literature, their own and their colleagues' past projects, and many other sources to help them along the way.

Depending on the time available, it may make sense to generate alternatives rather systematically from lists like those shown in Figure 3.2, but ultimately you must just sit down with a blank computer screen

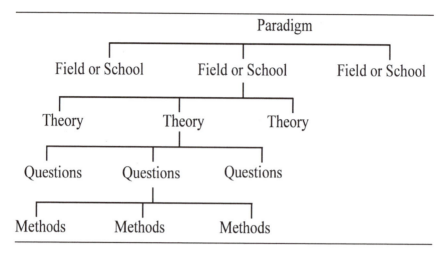

Figure 3.3. The Research Pyramid

or piece of paper and think of something you want to do that hasn't been done before, as far as you know.

EXERCISE 8

Generate five to ten ideas for writing projects.
Reduce them to your three top choices, synthesizing
your best ideas from the larger set.

Getting into a "rate busting" mentality is helpful to meet this assignment. Not too much detail is required. I ask that each idea be described in a paragraph or two. In addition to the basic topic, you should include at least three or four other project attributes: theoretic approach, population studied, ontological perspective, method of analysis, sources of data, audience addressed, and so on. Aim for variety on these dimensions as you move from one writing possibility to another. For example, think one day about great data sources; begin the next day by thinking about the theoretic perspectives that interest you most.

As you work on generating a larger pool of alternatives than most people consider explicitly, you may need some help following the "no evaluation" rule of brainstorming. I give this piece of advice:

⁄⁄   ⁄⁄

Establish a "bottom drawer" to file project
possibilities. Wait until you have a half-dozen or so
before you synthesize and evaluate them.

⁄⁄⁄

The bottom drawer of your desk has several attractive features as a research tool. First, you can and should keep the drawer shut most of the time, opening it only long enough to throw in your latest idea. It's not a very formal filing system, which is all to the good. You can even put in a book or picture or newspaper article that you find evocative.

Think about making this drawer a permanent part of your work environment. I find that I frequently have ideas for new projects throughout the research and writing process. They are not just research and writing ideas but teaching and other possibilities as well. Unfortunately, they often distract me from the work at hand. I take advantage of the intrinsic generative nature of scholarship by writing a brief description of each possibility as it intrudes upon me. Then, I file it in my bottom drawer for later consideration. Having done that, I can usually ignore what is otherwise an attractive nuisance.

You should wait at least until day five to open your bottom drawer and examine the results of your brainstorming efforts. Typically, I have to use a second critical research tool, the dining room table, to spread these papers out and categorize them. When I do that, I typically remain enthused about some possibilities that were in my mind all week, but I also see patterns that were not so obvious. I'm surprised, for example, by how often I return to a particular finding or refer to a particular article. Waiting to accumulate a set of possibilities thus lets me learn new things about myself.

Seeing my brainstorming efforts fresh, as a set, also makes it more likely that I'll see connections among my ideas. Brainstorming philosophy includes the idea that a first pass rarely produces a fully realized idea. You haven't finished with Exercise 8 until you consider combinations of ideas and select the most promising for discussion with others.

Four Parameters for Evaluating Research Topics

You move out of brainstorming into a very different logic when you begin to choose among alternatives. The more energy you put into generating research ideas, the more work you will have to do to reduce them to one choice and commit to writing one thing, now. The process of thinking about the merits of more than one genuine alternative, however, has multiple benefits. First, considering serious alternatives will give you confidence that you are choosing the best project to pursue as well as information about what aspects of this project are particularly important to you. Second, deliberately choosing among alternatives makes it less likely that another commitment or opportunity will derail you. Care in the choice of a project will also help develop a sense of your place in your field of scholarship, something that is harder to see as you move into the minutiae of writing. Finally, considering viable alternatives will help you establish a portfolio of research objectives that will both balance and diversify your work over time.

I do have an important suggestion for evaluating the alternatives you have chosen, but it is highly systematic. Indeed, I am following a very systematic template throughout this book. I have mixed feelings about this, because I know from my own research and writing experience that there are many aspects of choice, including happenstance, emotion, politics, and other forces that are not easily incorporated into a rational format. I'll discuss a few of these issues, but I urge you to focus on the "critical diamond" shown in Figure 3.4. It is the best tool I know to identify projects that are interesting, important, and likely to be published.

The scholar. Start evaluating alternatives by considering yourself. You must decide how much innate, not totally rational, enthusiasm you

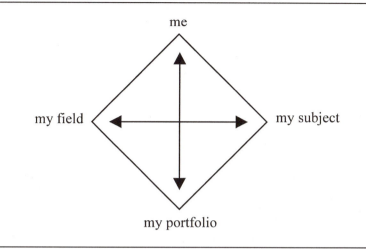

Figure 3.4. A "Critical Diamond" for Evaluating Writing (or Research) Alternatives

have for each serious possibility you have identified. Remember that scholarship is essentially a lonely activity. Most projects take longer than you estimate they will. Therefore, even when thinking about coauthoring, it doesn't make sense to work on a project if you don't like it. So, begin with your own interests.

There is an important balance to consider as you think about what you most want to do:

- Some projects are attractive because they fit your current skills and abilities. You are more likely to make a genuine contribution to your field if you emphasize your strengths. You also speed and simplify execution of the project.

- Other projects contribute to your development as a scholar, thus making subsequent projects more powerful. This is a key consideration for every scholar because it is our responsibility to invest in and develop our skills.

I don't have any easy metric to decide among projects, but I encourage you to weigh the merits of each project you consider along this difficult continuum, and I have this strongly felt piece of advice:

⁂

Do what really interests you—within reason.

⁂

Projects that codify or test what my mother already knows (and my mother knows a lot) are problematic. Life is short. Outcomes, including fame, are very difficult to predict. It therefore makes a lot of sense to me that each scholar should try to answer questions that genuinely perplex him or her. They will enjoy the process of scholarship and care less about the vagaries of publication. Projects that seek to "prove" something the author already believes are rarely of interest to me and probably are not of great interest to the author.

The field. You must also think about how interesting your possible writing project is to your field. This is as important as thinking about your own interest in the project. Consider a potential project's fit with dominant paradigms, currently "hot" topics, questions pursued by leaders in the field, understood methodologies, familiar sources of data, and so on.

Again, there is no easy metric. A project that is too far from the center of a field will have difficulty attracting attention and being understood. One that is too close to what has been done before is unlikely to be considered an interesting contribution to conversation. I have three pieces of advice:

- Make sure you are aware of current conversations. This is more easily done by following Internet conversations, working papers, conference proceedings and specialty meetings than by reading journals and books. The works now becoming available in published form were done at least two years ago; often they have had a much longer gestation period.
- Don't jump on today's "bandwagon" unless you feel you have an innate understanding of why it is interesting and important. Fads in most fields move fast. If you have an intrinsic understanding of your subject, you will be able to reframe it in terms of new enthusiasms if necessary.
- Finally, be expansive.

⁘   ⁘

Put all your relevant ideas into your
current project; do not ration good ideas in the hope
of second publication.

⁙⁙

The publications that make an impact are rarely one thin slice from a larger pie. Furthermore, new ideas will grow out of working with the ones you have. You therefore not only write a more interesting paper by working without constraint, you create the ground for additional interesting papers.

The subject. Even if your project involves historical data, it is good advice to consider what can be learned from the subject of study itself. There are at least three things to consider before embarking on a project:

- The intrinsic need for the study/article
- Site access
- Availability of data

Many insightful scholarly contributions begin with the observation of an anomaly in the world, a question about why something doesn't happen, or a revealing comparison among different data points. You can make a contribution if you codify what exists; you also can contradict current wisdom. You might ask a few people close to the subject what they think of your writing alternatives and how they would rank them. If you can capture their enthusiasm, you are far more likely to have an interesting story to tell.

Portfolio. Any one writing project is advanced at the expense of other alternatives, whether we pay much attention to them or not. When I get enthusiastic about a new project without thinking about the other things on my writing agenda, however, I often find that I lose time later. Often I have to suspend work to honor other commitments, or a cooler look at other options may push the interloper out of the picture altogether. Thinking in terms of a portfolio will help you avoid this misdirected effort. Time is your most precious resource. Most of us can think of many more possibilities than we will ever have time to complete, even with the help of coauthors.

The criteria for managing a set of promising projects depend upon many things—your field, your nonwriting responsibilities, your aspirations, where you are in your career. Some people seek variety and are happiest advancing many different interests at once. Others are much more disciplined, seeking significant influence on a specific conversation, perhaps working on one manuscript at a time. At issue is not only the range of subjects you choose to pursue, or how many endeavors you keep going at the same time, but where you will carry out the conversations that interest you.

The criteria for tenure and promotion are an obvious guide when making such decisions, but choices are often simplified and distorted by the academic grapevine. Few employment or promotion decisions are made solely on the basis of the number of publications in top journals, for example, as often believed in North America. It is obviously desirable to have been accepted in such outlets, but the cumulative impact and future trajectory of scholarly work is more important.

My point is that it makes sense to have an agenda and a timetable. I made a smart move as an associate professor, for instance, by editing a book in a new area of inquiry. However, it took a lot longer than I expected, and I wouldn't recommend working on a book without careful consideration. This is just one complexity that leads me to strongly recommend discussing the course you are charting with other people—not only senior advisers but peers who will see issues of immediate relevance that older colleagues may not notice. A plan will help you make the best decision about whether or not you can afford to work on the one project that is in the center of your radar screen at the moment.

You may discover you have too few choices. I find that many people have difficulty coming up with more than one *real* alternative from Exercise 8. I know this is true because when I ask people, "Which one of these three alternatives do you really want to write about?" they can usually tell me without a moment's hesitation. My advice to them is to go back to the brainstorming process and come up with more than one real candidate. Typically, they do this by becoming more micro, developing variations around what they now know they really want to do. That is fine. Just remember that you haven't really chosen your research project until you've felt some anguish over deciding what to do.

But, if you have gotten this far, it is equally likely that you have more ideas than time and resources. You may feel frustrated having to choose among one or more projects that vitally interest you, one or more that you think would most interest colleagues, or are compelling in terms of the subject matter itself. One way to ease this dilemma is to remember that the writing (or research) project you choose now is not the only thing you will work on over the next period of time.

Thinking in portfolio terms should help you balance a relatively high-risk project with other lower risk projects. "Risk" is something you will have to define for yourself, although some obvious dimensions include the predicted length of time to project completion, distance from central interests in your field, sensitive or low data availability, high cost—the list can go on and on. My rather obvious advice will have to be tailored to each individual's circumstances and career goals:

- Keep the pipeline full by considering the time requirements of different projects.
- Mix coauthored projects with projects done alone.
- Mix projects of great personal but low field appeal with "sure hit" projects.

Choose to Begin

The basic idea is that you must consider and reconsider your interests, the current conversation in your field, the issues raised by the subject, and the portfolio of your other projects until you feel comfortable that the writing project you are about to choose makes sense from all four points of the critical diamond. The choice among viable alternatives will thus not be easy, but it will be a real one.

EXERCISE 9

Evaluate your top three possibilities for research or writing on the four points of the critical diamond. After discussing your alternatives with others, commit to one project as the focus of your immediate attention.

A small bit of advice from the brainstorming literature here: Make your choices an exercise in deletion. Combine and synthesize ideas that come out of your Exercise 8 efforts, then decide which is least viable, interesting, and so on. Take that out of the pool, then delete the next least attractive.

Why focus on three choices for more detailed comparison? Because it is hard to discuss many more than three with other people. Collapsing to two, on the other hand, invites dichotomous thinking that will tend to overly simplify your choices.

As you make your final decision, I have a last piece of advice:

❧   ☙

Be interesting, but don't try to be avant-garde on every dimension.

❧❧❧❧

In the early flush of enthusiasm, with relatively little real information to disconfirm hope, it is easy to design a high-risk project. People with a certain turn of mind are likely to be lured by their opportunities. Excited by a new innovative-but-untested set of ideas, they get in over their heads methodologically or theoretically or just in terms of project scale. Other people, driven by the need to be different, may choose the radical alternative on as many dimensions of their work as possible. If your aim is to find an audience, both inclinations are problematic; your most distinctive contribution can be easily lost in the "white noise" of other distractions.

Some middle ground makes sense, for most people, most projects, most of the time. You have the greatest chance of being part of a scholarly community if you strive to be interesting and innovative, adding something new that has not been done before but within sight of the current boundaries of the field.

It is fun to try to push those boundaries. If you want to do that, my advice is to look for fellow travelers but simultaneously define a project that will be more easily understood by mainstream scholars. This work is most likely to bring you into conversation, which can help you be a successful revolutionary.

Continuing to Manage Your Portfolio

Your portfolio of research and writing projects will require continuing attention because its very existence can slow or even stop publication. Most ideas in your bottom drawer must stay in your bottom drawer. You must always make careful decisions about what you will work on now and what you line up for subsequent attention.

A feasible number of projects is not the only thing you must manage. If you do not think about your portfolio, you may find that you inadvertently talk to groups outside of your field about subjects that do not represent your primary interests but nonetheless lead to writing commitments. Increasing pressures to publish make these or other "quick hits" alluring. Three things must be kept in mind before taking the bait. The work you do now develops reputation and skills for the work you can most easily do next. Your list of publications and work in progress is a signal that others use to make decisions that can affect your career—sometimes you are not even aware they are being made. Finally, if your true passion lies elsewhere, you are wasting time.

Even when you remain focused, writing itself can create imbalance. Almost every project encounters difficulties. Analysis may be difficult; writing about limitations may be discouraging; an inviting introduction may be elusive. With experience, I have found some of these problems quite predictable. Certain parts of writing are hard to do, and turning attention to another paper is very appealing, especially one that is easier and more fun to work on. If you do not resist this temptation, your portfolio will suffer. You will move further and further from publication as the papers you have in hand require skills you have never developed.

Other emotions can also lead to uneven effort. One of the biggest mistakes I made in my early career was not to revise two different articles for the most prestigious journal in my field. Reviewers of the first work did not seem to understand my purpose. Their suggestions confused me, and I had grown tired, so I gave the paper to a friend working on an edited volume. A year later, I submitted a paper that was even more important to me. One reviewer wanted me to consider another literature, and the journal editor agreed. That made me mad. I had looked at that literature and found it less useful than the one I used as a foundation for my arguments. So I sent the second paper to a less widely circulated journal. Both were bad decisions, made without managerial oversight, that reduced the "value" of my portfolio of publications. With the 20/20 vision of hindsight, I should have asked other people to help me understand the first reviews. The second paper would have been stronger if I had added my impassioned argument for the greater utility of my literature over others and sent it back for reconsideration. I wasn't thinking in terms of conversation, and I ended up not reaching the audience that I most wanted to discuss my work.

A portfolio can help you initiate multiple conversations—but not too many. Although I am going to keep my attention focused on supporting your effort to get one manuscript to the point of submission, I encourage you to actively manage a limited and focused portfolio of scholarly effort so that other scholars have the opportunity to share and shape the knowledge you are gaining.

Conclusion

One of the reasons I had a hard time getting published after I received my PhD was that I could not decide *what* out of all the many things I might do, I wanted to do most. The critical diamond I've just described helped me balance the forces that pulled me in different directions. An ongoing portfolio of projects, some under way, others mere possibilities in my bottom drawer, has helped me work on *one* writing project right now, although in truth I continue to overcommit myself. In the hope that you can be more disciplined than I sometimes am, the rest of this book focuses on helping you "frame" and publish the project you chose in Exercise 9.

Note

1. Koberg, D., & Bagnall, J. (1976). *The universal traveler.* New York: William Kaufman.

Chapter 4

❦

Identifying Conversants

The idea that scholarship depends upon interaction with other scholars is widely accepted but often forgotten in the research and writing process. This chapter therefore coins the term "conversants" to identify specific written works that the author hopes to directly engage with his or her writing. Identifying three or four conversants (ideally before research begins but certainly before writing begins):

- *Will focus the questions asked, and influence the way they are answered, and*
- *Make publication more likely, if the rules of good conversation are followed*

Definitions

The first chapter of this book argues that scholarship is socially defined. This idea is well established in the sociology of science; a few salient references can be found in the bibliography. My definition of conversation is consistent with that literature.

Conversation is an inclusive term that covers many different forms of interaction among scholars. Although face-to-face discussion is an important part of that interaction, and informal electronic communications are increasingly important, the written word is still the primary mode of scholarly communication. All forms of communication transmit ideas and organizing influences, but articles and books are the more formal, more definitive statements intended to influence other scholars. This is an author's best forum for making an enduring contribution to scholarship.

When I speak of a *conversant*, I mean a specific article or book, a specific contribution to the canon of scholarly work in your field. I know I'm using formal, even sanctimonious language here. I think that scholarly work can and should influence others. That cannot be achieved if we don't take ourselves and our work seriously. Identifying specific conversants is a means to that end.

Active scholars write many statements, about many things. This complexity may be at the back of your mind, but I recommend that you isolate three or four written documents that are the most germane to what you hope to accomplish in a specific piece of work. As a set, these conversants may not come from one subdiscipline, with highly overlapping references; however, interacting references indicate you are on the right track—a conversation is going on.

Even if they do not reference each other, you should be able to imagine the authors in face-to-face conversation (whether or not this would be historically possible) and you should be able to imagine yourself as part of that conversation. Enormous advantage can be gained by the scholar who thus identifies precisely which works define the conversation they wish to join. For example, the image of face-to-face conversation with authors who have written specific articles or books helps edit my tendency to begin a writing project with too many different ideas in mind. I sometimes literally tack conversant papers on the bulletin board above my desk. As I begin to write, they curb my tendency to put in too many references, too many idiosyncratic enthusiasms that are tangential to my main point.

Good Conversation Tends
to Follow a Few Rules

As you know, the foundation of this book is the idea that good conversation promotes good scholarship—more specific targets for research, more current methods, more appropriate analysis, more germane referencing, more interesting theoretic development. These lofty goals are realized not only because people share and build on each other's ideas but because they energize and motivate each other. The bibliography lists a few recent works that extol the virtues of this kind of scholarly conversation.

Guidelines from these and other sources bear repeating.

1. *Listen before you speak.* Polite conversationalists do not walk up to a group and begin talking. Even if they are quite familiar with the individuals they approach, they wait to find out what is being discussed at the moment. The analogue in written conversation is to actually *read* and *reread* your conversant works, and make genuine connections with the important points being made. We all confuse making a copy of an article with reading and thinking about its contents. We are not in conversational mode when we forget to take seriously what has already been said.

2. *Connect with points already made.* Inept conversationalists make a passing reference to the current conversation but move quickly to what they had on their minds before joining the group. The more interesting conversationalist continues to make genuine links to the ideas of others. As a result, the content they intended to share upon arrival is shaped by the conversation, and shapes the conversation. By extension, the generation of new ideas that could only have come from engaging with others is the sign of successful scholarship.

3. *Be interesting.* We don't listen long to those who repeat previous points in a conversation or are tangential to the main thread of conversation. The good conversationalist thinks about the people he or she is talking to, considers what would interest them, edits content to make sure that these connections are clear, and then says something the others have not thought of before.

I don't mean to set the hurdle too high or to discourage you from enthusiastically pursuing a scholarly project. Just keep this thought in mind: Write as if you were speaking to the people you would most like to meet. If you were lucky enough to meet an author in the conversation that interests you, you would not be completely tongue-tied but would work hard to think of the most interesting thing you could say. You would try to avoid saying what they already know.

4. *Be polite.* The norms of conversation differ, with some groups encouraging a level of repartee and conflict that others would find intolerable, but every conversation has its boundaries. In my opinion,

newcomers in particular are well advised to consider and remain within these boundaries. The desire to be noticed, the hope of saying something interesting, and the bravado required to speak up can push one beyond the norms of good conversation. It's a high-risk strategy.

It Is Important to Identify
Specific Conversants

I hope you are convinced about the utility of the conversational metaphor. It is a metaphor in the sense that you can imagine yourself at the door of a crowded room of conversing scholars (present and past) in the process of choosing which group you want to join. It is more than a metaphor given that you can trace the volley of ideas from one article or book to another and see the shaping influence of that interaction. Exercise 10 invites you to do just that:

EXERCISE 10

*Identify the three or four written works that you would like to be
the primary conversants for your paper.*

In my experience, this is not an easy exercise. Not only do referencing habits (especially in North America) obscure the main thread of a conversation, most scholars are interested in many different topics and additions that distract from their primary message. This is precisely why it is important to force yourself to focus on a very limited set of works as the foundation for each writing project you undertake. I encourage you to

- Weed out conversants that define a large field and look instead for those written about a specific question that interests you.
- Choose conversants that you find most interesting, even though you do not necessarily agree with the points made, rather than conversants that support your point of view but do not add much to it (be careful

though—if someone has already said what you want to say, you need to rethink your contribution).

- Include a new voice or two in your conversant list but lean toward well-known works that a broader audience will recognize and find interesting.

Perhaps the biggest problem arises when you wish to draw on more than one field of inquiry. For example, the subject of your intended research may be defined by your major field of training, but you want to borrow a theoretic idea from a second field and/or use a method developed in a third. The idea of scholarship as conversation has been most helpful to me in these circumstances. It is tempting to be sidetracked into thinking that you should publish a paper in field two, illustrating the application of their theory to the population you have studied. Or you may be very excited about your success in fine-tuning your methodology, and think that other people using that method might be interested in your work. These thoughts are most often siren songs; they have tempted many to stray off course and dilute the potential impact of their work. My advice is simple:

Identify conversants that will help you focus on your main field of scholarship!

The authors of these works are the people you have been trained to talk with. They are the people you are most likely to continue to talk with. Your first objective must be to convince them that your insight is of importance for understanding your mutual area of interest.

After you have done that, you can think about branching out to other disciplines, but note that you will have to orient your writing toward the conversation going on in the new field, and must choose conversants from that field. It's a lot of work and less likely to be successful if you do not have the requisite training or background. You'll have to decide whether it is worth it to you, or whether you would rather work on another project that further advances your main line of inquiry.

Conversants Focus Both
Research and Writing

The primary benefit of identifying conversants before you go too far in defining a specific writing project has to do with purposefully grounding your efforts in a specific scholarly conversation. Knowing who you want to talk to helps clarify research choices and is especially helpful as you begin to define exactly what you want to write about. I think it helps authors develop a more interesting and forceful "voice." Now is the time to start, even though you have to speculate and will need to continue reviewing the match between your conversants and your message as you write more.

EXERCISE 11

Identify the three or four findings from your scholarly work that would interest the conversants you have identified.

Some people have a very hard time with this exercise, although others are blessed by relatively well-organized fields of inquiry that make the choices rather obvious. If you had difficulty, spend some time reading recent journals and books, asking yourself, "What do I have to say about this?" You'll find that you have little to add to some work, even though it may interest you. In other cases, you are likely to have a more active response. When you wish you could spend some time debating about the points being made, you have a potential conversant.

Figure 4.1 may be of interest, whether or not you resort to the literature. Creating such a matrix can be very helpful even for those who did not have much trouble identifying conversants because they still

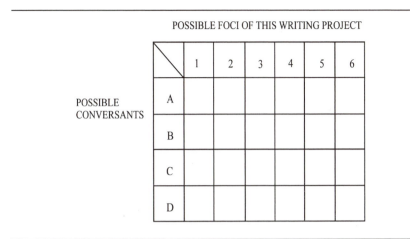

POSSIBLE FOCI OF THIS WRITING PROJECT

	1	2	3	4	5	6
A						
B						
C						
D						

POSSIBLE CONVERSANTS

Figure 4.1. Alternative Definitions of a Research Project

have to choose what they most want to say. Once again, it is helpful to make some decisions before wasting writing time.

If you have difficulty defining the work you want to do, I have this suggestion:

Getting mad can help you make choices.

There is always more than one group that might be interested in your project. There are always several ways you could present your work, even to one group. With a little heat, you may discover who you really want to talk to and what you most want to say. Pretend you are being ignored. Pretend you have to shout to be heard. Pretend you can send only one brief telegraph message from the other side of the world. Now, what are you going to say?

Identify Target Journals
After Choosing Conversants

I believe that it is better to choose the outlet for your written work after you have identified the conversation you wish to join and the major points you wish to make. The journal influences the way you "phrase" your message; it does not dictate the message or the audience. In fact, there is almost always more than one choice of publishing outlet, although the range of alternatives depends upon the field.

EXERCISE 12

Identify a primary and a secondary target journal.
Copy the first page of several articles from each
journal that interests you.

Discuss the logic of your choices with others,
using the first pages as evidence.

It makes sense to consider the unique "flavor" of the journal you hope will publish your work before you begin to write. This outlet has a history. The current editor probably has some sense of the articles he or she would like to see, although my experience has been that virtually all editors welcome a wide range of contributions, often wider than they in fact receive. If you skim several recent volumes of your target journal, especially those that reflect the choices of the current editor, you can make sure your intended contribution fits this venue. Once again, you are trying to save time before you begin to write. Spare a bit of attention too for your second choice. If you do not succeed with your first submission, you will more easily maintain your momentum with a second choice in mind.

Conclusion

I hope that the last discussion of target journals did not confuse your understanding of conversants. The basic point of this chapter is to focus your attention on a small set of written works that most directly precede and influence your own. If you would like to influence the authors of these works (whether or not this is historically possible), you have found your conversants. After doing that, you can choose the setting within which the conversation might take place.

Once you've committed yourself to a small specific set of conversants and have a basic idea of the contribution you would like to make to their conversation, you have a useful blueprint for how to proceed. I hope that you had some images of those you wished to engage from the beginning of your research, because any work of scholarship is likely to interest some groups of conversants more than others. As you begin writing, it is time to check this image and make it more explicit for the specific aspect of the work you are reporting.

Chapter 5

❖

Using Exemplars

There is no reason to reinvent the wheel when writing, especially because scholarly conversations typically follow conventions that facilitate clear communication. "Exemplars" can be used to speed the scholar's understanding of these conventions. This chapter defines exemplars and suggests that they:

- *Help authors define their purpose more clearly*
- *Can be used to structure and solve problems in writing*
- *Are a springboard for innovating beyond the structures used by others*

Definition

An *exemplar* is a document already in the literature that accomplishes the kind of task you are trying to accomplish *in an effective way*. It does not have to address the subject that interests you. In fact, it is often helpful to look for examples of similar work outside your immediate domain of interest.

It has been said that imitation flatters the person whose work is copied; it also saves the imitator's time. Exemplars of scholarly writing provide ideas for approaching unfamiliar communication tasks. When you are unsure of how to present your material, how much background to give, or how much detail to furnish, exemplars provide a compendium of possible solutions. They offer especially useful instruction on completing the most important task of scholarship—making sure that your contribution to knowledge is clearly stated.

In other words, recipes for almost every type of scholarly writing you can imagine already exist. When you search for exemplars, you are looking to your predecessors for instruction.

The careful scholar might worry about plagiarism. Replicating another's work is plagiarism, which is a serious offense because it erodes the trust necessary for scholarly conversation to take place. I do not believe the use of exemplars that I will suggest is a problem. You bring your own perspective to everything you write, and your unique subject matter will put its own distinctive stamp on what you write. I recommend using exemplars because it is useful to follow basic conventions, yet few of us are as knowledgeable about those conventions as we might be.

I first learned about exemplars when faced with a grant proposal deadline. I had a good idea, but I was unsure about how to develop it because I had never written a proposal before. One of my colleagues had been successful in a previous competition, and when I asked for a copy of his proposal, he generously provided it. Of course I didn't have much time; out of ignorance and desperation I started by deliberately mimicking the way he had structured his proposal. His summary had three paragraphs, moving from the general to the specific. Therefore so did mine. Of course, it wasn't possible to keep this up. I wrote three introductory paragraphs to his two and could only think of three contributions of my study, even though he had five. He didn't have a future projects section, but I thought that was critical to my proposal, and so on.

In short, the structure was *very* useful to me, but my ideas and materials quickly began to take over. The exemplar was a great way to get started, and a very useful platform for moving into my own work, because I understood more quickly what I needed to do.

It is not essential to the story that I got funded, but I did. I think one reason for my success was that I was able to sound sure of myself. Even more important, I had a first lesson in the judo of scholarship. By understanding the way in which things had been successfully done before, I could more precisely position myself to do something new.

It really does not make sense to start a scholarly project as if you were on a desert island. Virtually every kind of scholarly task has been tried before—sometimes more successfully than others. To find a good example that you can learn from, however, you first must define what you are trying to do.

Step 1: Specify Your Intent

A useful statement of purpose is more detailed than "Write a case study," but it does not have to be complex. What do you hope to add to the literature with your case study (or whatever)? A sufficient elaboration might read:

1. Describe the behavior I observed, which is not easily explained by current theory.
2. Focus attention on the unusual environmental forces that may have elicited that behavior.
3. Outline a set of questions for the reader to consider.

The objective of an alternative article from the very same inquiry might be as follows:

1. Review current theory about X.
2. Focus on recent studies that suggest weaknesses in that theory.
3. Summarize perplexing empirical evidence from my case study.
4. Outline an agenda for further study.

Note that the first set of objectives is likely to yield a different paper than the second. Even if both are based on the same research and hope to reach the same audience, they are somewhat different contributions and will require different structures. Discussion of the literature will predominate in the second effort and perhaps be totally absent in the first. The second is likely to be rather formal, while the first is likely to be more conversational. Clearly, it would be helpful to make a deliberate decision before beginning to write.

EXERCISE 13

*Describe what you hope to accomplish in your
writing project in at least three different ways.*

Settle on one succinct description.

*Seek advice about this objective from advisers and
your writing community.*

I ask the people who work with me to seek exemplars because
I have seen the attempt to identify the type of paper to be written
bring benefits even before the author finds a single exemplar. In the
effort to carry out Exercise 13, many scholars just beginning to write
discover that (a) they do not have a very clear idea of *what* they want
to communicate, (b) they are trying to do too much or too little,
(c) they are not focusing on what they are able to do best, and/or
(d) what they first propose to do is not the most interesting thing they
could do.

If one or more of these vexing conclusions applies to you, do not
get overly discouraged. The work you are doing, or have done, can be
communicated in many different ways, to many different audiences.
You need to find the right way of framing the writing task as well as the
right audience. Perhaps you will decide that more research is necessary
to write the paper you envision; making that assessment now means
you will not waste time on a writing project that is unlikely to reach
fruition. Thus do not move beyond this exercise just because it brings
painful news. *Now is the time to identify a clear and viable goal*—before *you
begin to write.*

However, I hesitate to advise you to have a clear goal in mind before
you begin to write. Some people feel that if they have to know what
they are going to do, they will never start. In Appendix A, Mary Jo Hatch
makes a good case for just beginning to write and discovering the shape
of your paper as you move along. Only you can decide if this approach
will work for you, or whether you are likely to start out with a debili-
tating lack of direction.

Step 2: Choose Published Examples of Work With a Similar Objective

One good test of whether you have defined a writing project that will easily communicate with other scholars is whether you can identify published work that has successfully accomplished the same kind of task. The most useful exemplars will probably be in the journal you are targeting. If you are thinking about a book, or a book chapter, the most useful exemplars are likely to have been accepted by the editor and/or published by the house you hope will accept your manuscript.

EXERCISE 14

Identify four or five exemplars of the kind of paper you want to write. If necessary, seek advice about the fit between these exemplars and your project, then settle on a final group of two or three works.

There are two potential benefits from a more explicit look at conventions around writing a certain kind of article, dissertation, or book. First, if you want to be an effective communicator within a scholarly group, it is useful to know and use established conventions. Second, deliberately avoiding convention is often the most effective way to surprise and inform that group.

The adage "garbage in, garbage out" should be kept in mind as you carry out this exercise. Be sure you have found exemplars that can be admired for how they discuss a project similar to your own. Many things are published that are not exemplary! In addition, remember that you do not need to worry about finding exemplars in your particular subject of study. An exemplar is used for insight into *how* something is done, not what to do—that must come from you.

Step 3: Examine the Structure
and Tone of Successful Exemplars

When you look for exemplars, you are looking for instruction in the "rules of the game." These shared conventions are an important aspect of what makes conversation possible across time and space. Every social endeavor is influenced by tacit assumptions and codes of behavior. Often these are not obvious to a newcomer. Even scholars who have been part of a group for a while will probably not notice all the conventions that underlie published work.

To make the tacit more explicit, I recommend the following:

EXERCISE 15

*Outline in detail each exemplar in your
final set, noting the proportion of the
text devoted to each topic.*

*Also make notes about the "tone" used
in your exemplar.*

*Draw conclusions about the tacit rules for this kind of
contribution to scholarly conversation.*

People who formally analyze a set of articles in this way are typically surprised by how much commonality they find, especially because they are looking at works on different subjects, possibly published in different outlets. The order of presentation is often standardized; the size of different components, like the literature review or the discussion of findings, is often quite similar. You may even note similarities in smaller details, like the use of examples. These commonalities are what I mean by the "rules of the game."

Following such conventions is not mandatory, but my advice is that if you choose not to follow the rules, you should have good reasons. When you present your work in the way people expect, they tend to feel that you know what you are doing and you gain credibility. Readers can more easily remember what you have said and anticipate what you will discuss next. Why challenge these assumptions unless you have a reason for doing so? Save your capacity to surprise for a part of the paper that has the content to surprise.

You also have to keep your internal compass in working order. Although an exemplar may be effective as a whole, it is unlikely to be equally effective in each thing it tries to accomplish. Thus it is useful to take a more fine-grained look at your set of exemplars.

EXERCISE 16

Identify the aspects of each exemplar that are particularly effective as well as any that are ineffective in communicating the author's purpose.

Step 4: Move Beyond Your Exemplars

In the next few chapters, I will suggest that you turn again and again to your exemplars for advice about how to proceed. Every aspect of these papers, from title to references, is a potential source of help in your writing project. Not only the overall outline, but very specific details, like the structure of topic sentences, the number of examples offered, even the tense and length of sentences are a potential source of help. Even in the areas where it is not totally effective, an exemplar can be useful because it pushes you to more clearly articulate what you think *will* be meaningful.

The goal, however, is to go beyond mechanically copying these examples. Use your analysis to identify where you are making a unique contribution to the literature and think about ways to usefully depart from your exemplars to more effectively deliver the primary message of your paper.

One important caution: When looking at other work, you will see things that you wish you had done. Not only do they seem to exemplify good scholarship, the fact that what you are reading is published might be taken as a sign that certain things are required. Writing is a simplification anyway, and often ideas and actions are presented out of their historical sequence. It can seem an easy step to add a hypothesis you did not have, introduce a literature you had not considered, or otherwise "doctor" what you are working with. I have a very important piece of advice.

⁂

Never lie. Say exactly what you did, and why.

⁂

My mother used to say that one of the problems with a lie is that it often requires another lie to sustain it, and then another. The same is true of academic writing. The small deviation from what actually was done can seem pretty trivial at the time. It may even slip in unnoticed by the unpracticed author trying to muscle a manuscript into published form. But the tidying addition often makes later steps less logical or plausible; deceit must escalate or the written account starts to dissolve.

My strong advice is to hold yourself rigorously to describing what you did, explaining what you wish you had done if absolutely necessary. Often your reason is good enough to meet scholarly standards. If not, go back to work and get it right. Just raise your hand and take the pledge to tell the truth; you will be saved doubt and difficulty, and make an honest contribution to scholarship.

Conclusion

As you know, I believe strongly in creating a community of other people who will offer you advice on various aspects of your writing efforts. Exemplars are a very useful adjunct to this group of people who have their own lives to lead and will not always be available to you. When you are working quickly, exemplars can offer immediate advice, even in the middle of the night. As the manuscript lengthens, exemplars can minimize the burden you ask others to bear. The human adviser has to "get into" the project and may have to read a substantial portion of the manuscript to understand even a very specific question. Because they have a similar agenda, your exemplars can offer concrete advice on the way you might handle things that perplex you.

As you move through the following chapters, I will suggest that you may need to look for "mini-exemplars" as well. If you run into roadblocks as you write, the first place to look for advice is the set of exemplars you have just established. But if you still are having difficulty, it may be useful to seek additional guidance, perhaps from papers that are not that similar in overall format. For example, if you are challenging a major figure in the field, or presenting weak but, you hope, provocative research results, advice can be found in a wide range of sources. In working with these additional exemplars, follow the steps in this chapter: Find good examples, examine their structure and tone, then adapt the format to your own paper. In the process, you are likely to come up with something that is uniquely, and effectively, your own.

Part III

❧❧

Basic Components of Scholarly Writing

The chapters in this part of the book march through the generic parts of a scholarly paper. Many writers do not follow the sequence I establish in these chapters. Nonetheless, I argue that it is usually time-consuming to postpone working on title, abstract, and introduction—subjects of the first three chapters that follow. Thinking about these summarizing components of scholarly writing helps calibrate your efforts. Advice from various sources can help you in that task, and advice is much easier to get when you are working on these shorthand summaries.

Subsequent chapters discuss writing and presenting the work as a whole, getting it out for review, revision, and resubmission. Of necessity, the advice cannot be complete. Each field has its own conventions. Success with your project may involve analysis I don't even mention. But do read the last chapter on revision and submission. It is intended to support your confidence and enthusiasm until you reach publication.

Chapter 6

⁘

Title and Abstract

Now at last it is time to actually begin writing. People differ in their approach, so any one of the next chapters might be the starting point that best suits you and the project you intend to bring to publication. Wherever you start, you will almost certainly cycle through all aspects of your paper many times.

Nonetheless, I believe the title and abstract of a paper are its anchor points and worth early detailed attention. These two small parts of the paper:

- *Attract the "right" audience for your contribution*
- *Develop their interest in reading the work in its entirety*
- *Summarize your contribution to the literature in a way that readers—you hope—will remember, whether or not they read on*

Reviewing and reworking the title and abstract over time also will help clarify your own understanding of what you are presenting. Thus it is worth the time to carefully craft these statements.

Definitions

The *title* of a scholarly work has to represent the whole. It has the very difficult task of attracting the interest of busy and distracted scholars while also clearly specifying your subject so that your work shows up in the right databases and computer searches. In other words, the ideal title is both "hot" and "cold."

An *abstract* carries the same burden but has to deliver much more content. It is restricted to a few words, but the reader expects a summary

67

of what the paper achieves, not just a list of the major subjects covered. The task is still difficult and contradictory—you are trying to sell and inform, entice and codify.

Attracting the Right Readers
Will Depend on Title and Abstract

Writing is an act of communication. Communication has three essential parts: a sender, a receiver, and a message. Perhaps you are thinking to yourself that conversation is more fluid, that the "sender" and "receiver" are almost always in a dialogue that mixes these roles, that the message is transformed not only by who writes and who reads but by contexts within which the conversation takes place. All true. But written words, and even the words spoken in most scholarly settings, *are* linear. It is frustrating. There are some tricks to play that try to smooth the rough edges, but basically you are sending a message about something you have done or thought to a large number of other scholars. The place to begin, before you write, is to think about the nature of that audience.

❧   ❧

Imagine your readers. Put yourself in
their place.
This is your expanded set of conversants.

❧❧❧

My earlier advice to select a very limited set of conversants as the focal point of your paper is based on the belief that this commitment will focus your writing and make it more lively. I also believe that making a clear connection to a specific set of papers is most likely to attract a larger audience. Now it is important to consider that broader group of readers more explicitly. What are they interested in? What do they know already? What about your project will surprise and interest them? How are they likely to use the information you could provide? You may have to add some helpful asides to make sure that you are not excluding this group as you address your conversants.

I have found again and again that not being clear about my exact audience causes me trouble. As I finish this book, I am also trying to finish a book based on 10 years of research. My coauthor and I are ambitious and want to make a strong theoretic statement to the field as a whole. On the other hand, the topics we have investigated come out of a specific subfield, and most chapters reflect that focus. The question we are wrestling with is whether we want to address the whole field in the introduction and conclusion, or address the subfield that is most likely to be interesting, ending with a statement about our work's place in a larger agenda. The introductory chapter we envision is quite different in the first scenario than in the second. In fact, the collection of conversants shifts to some extent depending upon which path we take, and modest changes will take place in chapter emphasis. We should have made this decision long ago. I encourage you to be more proactive than we have been.

The title and abstract locate the work in a specific scholarly conversation but also try to appeal to the largest possible audience. Sometimes people begin too broadly, briefly attracting many unintended readers while almost certainly missing some who would be genuinely interested in the particular but hidden focus of the work. Others write in such specialized detail that they are unlikely to capture those who might be interested in broader implications. Authors who begin in the middle of a conversation also make it difficult for those who are not directly involved to understand what the paper is about and again decrease the potential audience.

Write an Informative Title

The title is your first effort to resolve these issues and reach your chosen audience. You must use words that will interest not only conversants but a larger group of readers, and avoid words that will bore them. Metaphors, puzzles, a play on words, even a song title, all seem attractive ways to accomplish the task. But you don't want to be too cute, and you must use words that will attract more pragmatic, often hurried, readers and suit the computer programs that are used for key word searches.

One of the more reliable ways I know to write an interesting title is to challenge reader expectations or current opinion in some credible way. For example, the title "An Agenda for Field X" would convey a bit more information if changed to "An International Agenda for Field X." It would be more interesting still if the author were ready to caution against "Wasting Resources on International Replication in Field X." It is hard to say more without knowing your field; just try to write a title that would start an interesting conversation.

Complicated scholarly projects need multiple words to represent their contents. Thus scholars are tempted into long titles, often separated by a colon to signal where the reader should catch a mental breath before plowing on. The obvious advice is to be as brief as you possibly can and hope you will have the opportunity to converse more fully with your readers as they move on to the body of the paper. A brief, informative, and memorable title is the marker for the conversation that can then take place. Ideally, it can be remembered without searching through stacks of papers or bibliographies; a long title is unlikely to move into long-term memory.

This is not an easy preface for an assignment, but it is time to begin writing.

EXERCISE 17

*Come up with at least three titles for
your work.*

*Under each, write at least two things in
favor of using the title and two things that make it
less suitable as the most salient representative of
your work.*

Discuss this list with others.

Then, decide on the working title of your paper.

Once again, I have found that it is often difficult for people actually to carry out this assignment; once again, I am arguing that by generating several viable alternatives and choosing among them, you will learn something about the paper you want to write.

Think About Key Words
Before Writing an Abstract

Some journals use key words to help focus attention on the major subjects of an article. Your target may not want a list, but it is still helpful to decide what your key words are.

EXERCISE 18

Even if your intended outlet does not require it, identify
three to five key words that convey the most
important topics of your paper.

Again, I am touting the benefits of decision. If you make a commitment to a specific vocabulary, you can use and develop these words throughout your paper to focus your attention as well as the reader's attention.

Summarize Your Contribution
to the Literature in the Abstract

As you move from title to abstract, keep thinking about attracting the interest of your audience while also getting as much essential information into the message as possible. This is not easy because now you must succinctly summarize what you have accomplished.

An abstract should do the following:

Provide further information about the main subjects covered in the paper.
A well-written abstract introduces the critical concepts in a paper; there

should be no surprises on page 17 caused by the introduction of a new literature and line of thinking.

Provide information about the type of contribution. Is this a theoretic or an empirical paper? Is it descriptive or prescriptive? Inductive or deductive? Some people will decide whether to read further based on these issues. Even more important, six months after they have read your article, they are more likely to use it again if the abstract includes descriptive detail.

Clearly indicate the contribution of the paper. There are obviously many different ways of writing a good paper, and some of the most memorable defy most of the "rules" I have and will put forth. Despite this disclaimer, one of the most important rules of abstracts, in my opinion, is to summarize, or at least give examples of, the most important contributions made. In other words, scholarly writing typically does not follow the mystery novel format in which the most important piece of information is withheld until the last few pages. The "whodunit" does occasionally appear in print, typically written by those least and most expert in the field. My advice is to learn how to lay your cards on the table before you move on to more difficult writing styles. You will thereby maximize the chances that you attract and hold a large audience.

With this short but difficult list established, it is time to write the abstract for your paper.

EXERCISE 19

Write an abstract of no more than 150 words for your paper.

You may have started this exercise with some confidence that you could at least write a short summary statement about a project you have been considering for some time; you probably ended with a more humble view of your abilities. Perhaps you felt unsure to begin with, and your first efforts didn't bolster your confidence. In either case, do not despair. As you continue, the title and abstract of your paper can and should be reworked. Doing so will remind you of the contributions you are trying to make; you will become more and more focused and persuasive as you continue to give them attention.

Edit for Clarity

After working for a while to include important information, you should try deleting the filler that almost always creeps into titles and abstracts. Following simple (but difficult) stylistic conventions will also attract readers and simplify computerized retrieval.

⁓ ⁓

- *Short sentences*
- *Present tense*
- *Active voice*
- *Simple constructions*
- *No more than two instances of the same word*

⁓⁓

These are rules from any basic speaking or writing course. Whether or not you have taken such a course, you know these rules. I know them. Sometimes it is helpful to break them; more often we lose conversational ground by not following them.

Think specifically about cutting out words or phrases as you work. When faced with a word limit, I am amazed by how much I can delete without significant loss of information. In fact, the titles, abstracts, and bodies of a paper often can be reduced by 30%-50% without serious loss. In a world of serious information overload, there are interesting computer programs that mechanically do just that. I understand they are quite effective. The reasons to edit oneself, before being mechanically slimmed, are twofold: It's a reader-friendly move, and it clarifies your basic purpose.

Once you begin to feel pretty confident, you might try this "acid test" before moving on:

EXERCISE 20

Give several strangers your title, abstract,
and key words.

Ask what they think your paper is about.

What would interest them most about such a paper?

This exercise gives you a better basis for judging whether you are trying to do too much or too little than just conversing with yourself. The time to realistically calibrate your effort is right now.

In addition, outsiders can help you "frame" your approach. Often a concept the author considers central and obvious confuses those outside the field; they don't understand it or they misinterpret it. Sometimes the author decides to stick with the original formulation, because targeted readers can be assumed to be familiar with the ideas being used. More often authors realize they are using vocabulary that only a few insiders could be expected to know. In this case, "the stranger test" can reorient the paper toward more central assumptions in the field and a wider audience, before you write any further.

Another serendipitous outcome of this exercise can be the discovery that parts of the project fascinate outsiders more than they have interested you. Typically, an author does not intend to write to people outside her or his field, because scholarship is a community activity. But discussion with people outside the field of inquiry—with nonacademics, partners, taxi drivers, and so on—can reenergize you, highlighting aspects of the project that deserve more emphasis, even for those within the field.

Conclusion

I ask people in my workshops to spend quite a lot of time on titles and abstracts because I believe that if they can express themselves clearly at this point in the writing process, they will save an enormous amount of effort in the writing that follows. Furthermore, they can easily ask for advice from others at this point. It is not that hard to read and comment on 150 words, and yet the conversation around those few words will focus on the core of the writing project ahead.

Despite these compelling points, if you can't write a good title and abstract, move on. There may be a better entry point to your paper; you can write the title and abstract later. But do not let yourself off the hook too easily. It would be a shame if halfway into the paper you finally write the abstract that pleases you, and then discover it requires you to dump ten pages of hard work.

Chapter 7

֍

Making an Outline (Really!)

I learned how to make an outline under Mrs. Rice's careful and demanding eye in seventh grade and did not write one again until years after getting my PhD, although of course I occasionally had to fake it by writing an outline after finishing a paper. Lately I've found them very useful and feel qualified to make the assertion that outlines do save time. Making an outline:

- *Allows the scholar to experiment with the order of presentation*
- *Accentuates the dominant features of the paper as the audience is likely to perceive them*
- *Helps the scholar define and highlight the value of the work being written*

Definition

An *outline* summarizes the order and logic of a written piece of work. It is the skeleton that supports audience understanding. By forcing authors to highlight major points and summarize the detail to be presented under each point, an outline also provides directions that reduce the need for constant inspiration as writing proceeds.

The logic of the outline need not be linear or nested—even impressionistic, emotional, and evocative writing benefits from "good bones." This chapter recommends giving deliberate attention to the structure of writing, whatever that structure is.

Why Take the Time to Outline?

A formal outline is not necessary for all scholarly writing. For example, you may not need to begin with an outline if you want to describe a research project you know in detail to an audience with little a priori knowledge of your subject. On the other hand, an outline in this circumstance can be as useful for suppressing unnecessary content as it is in other circumstances for organizing a complicated presentation of material. Similarly, if you have been teaching a subject in a structured way, you may not need to outline a written presentation of the same material. But again you should be careful. A change in audience or level of detail can make an outline useful.

In short, I have become suspicious of my tendency to dive into writing without an outline because I often waste time sorting out logic and detail in the middle of the project. As I've taken on more complex and ambitious writing tasks, I've found outlining essential to "keeping the story straight." The writing I want to accomplish is subtle; its density repays attention. Outlining doesn't make that happen, it just makes it possible.

Outlining is easier because I do not write a separate document with roman numerals before major headings, with secondary headings marked by the alphabet, and so on, and so on, as Mrs. Rice taught me. Instead, I work directly on the current draft of my paper, typically following these steps:

1. Begin with at least two and often three levels of headings, in bold, to mark the major structure of the paper. I often begin a paper by writing a paragraph or two of introduction. Then I play with various headings that mark the major subjects I intend to cover. I work with this structure until it gets more complicated. I don't start writing until I have some confidence that I have enough to say, although often my starting outline covers less than half of what I ultimately discuss. As I write more, I typically add headings and subheadings. How much detail I go into depends upon the difficulty of the project and its importance to me.

2. As the outline takes shape, check headings against the logic of the abstract (and introduction, once it is written). I have a strong sense of logic, but I am amazed at how often I catch inconsistencies in my early writing. Basic structural order is the beginning of logic in the argument itself; as the paper takes shape, I look for logic in details. The impact of scholarly writing is often carried by detail.

3. Write topic sentences before full text, especially in difficult sections of the paper. This piece of advice is the result of another flash of insight I couldn't believe had taken me so long to discover. As the product of a liberal arts college, I had considerable experience with different modes of writing and had gradually come to disdain straightforward structures, including subject-verb sentences and paragraphs led by a topic sentence. With experience, I have reverted to a more straightforward style as the best format for conveying complicated academic messages. In a busy world, where most academics (and even an occasional editor or reviewer) skim rather than read the many sources they need to follow, I believe that it make sense to submit to the discipline of a clear topic sentence framework.

Consult Your Exemplars' Outlines as a Useful Source of Outlining Advice

Basically, you are looking for a format, a logic, that fits the purpose and style of your paper. As already noted in Chapter 5, there is little reason to assume that the kind of writing you are attempting has never been done before; you should therefore seek an effective format in the exemplars you have collected.

Please note, however, that this is dangerous advice, because old structures can lure you into old messages. Your value to scholarly conversation depends upon your saying something new. Here's the judo trick you must try to perform:

⁕ ⁕

Be innovative with form and content, but only with a purpose.

⁕⁕⁕⁕

Do not wear your readers out trying to understand a strange order or unexpected argument unless you reward their effort. You risk losing their attention before payoff if you insist on unnecessary departures from the expectations of established discourse.

Use Your Outline to Highlight
What *You* Are Adding to the Literature

As I try to help my students with writing projects, I am constantly amazed by how hard it is to discover what is new about their writing project and what it contributes to the literature. It is quite common to find, toward the end of a long paragraph on page 5, after a long discussion of what other people have been doing, a short sentence or clause like the following: "This paper looks at three other variables: x, y, and z." The burial is complete when the paper goes on to discuss work that has already been done on x, y, and z.

Here's the remedy I suggest:

1. *Know how your paper makes a significant departure from the literature.* Mark that departure with a topic sentence at least—better yet, use a heading.

2. *Know why that departure is important and interesting to the conversation you are joining.* Make this part of the discussion of what you are doing, again using assertive topic sentences and headings.

3. *Make sure that you adequately discuss the implications of your work.* Don't assume that others will understand how they might use your work.

4. *Do not conclude with a discussion of your paper's limitations.* It is important to know and be clear about the boundaries of your study. However, you should not leave your reader mulling over the things you did not do; you want them to remember what you did.

The details depend upon the conversation you are a part of as well as the conventions of the journal or publisher you are targeting. After considering these details, I hope you will take my advice to resist the temptation to skip outlining and make one for yourself:

EXERCISE 21

Establish the major and secondary headings of your paper using tertiary headings as needed.

Seek advice on the logic, sequence, and emphasis of your outline from others.

Expand the introduction and conclusion by writing topic sentences for each paragraph.

Evaluate Your Outline From the Reader's Perspective

Whether or not you have access to a community that can give you personal feedback about your outline, and again I encourage you to make the effort to establish this worthwhile network, it is very important to make your own evaluation of the outline you have written. The price of later evaluation is high; there is still time to save time.

The essential framework for evaluation is the reader's reaction. The author and the reader are naturally aligned because they are part of the same conversation. They have similar or complementary backgrounds; they are interested in the same issues, fascinated by similar data and methods, likely to be convinced by similar kinds of arguments.

And yet, author and audience are very different. The author has just gone through a significant amount of work that readers have not shared. Typically, that work has altered and complicated his or her perspective, making it less like the reader's than it was before. This new difference is what makes communication worthwhile, but difficult. As a first step in realignment, I have an important piece of advice:

❖   ❖

Cut the first part of your outline.
Think about beginning with your current
conclusion.

❖❖❖

Many authors begin with too much background. They typically are attached to the historical process of discovery they went through, even though they recognize that it was an inefficient and tortuous path. Further, they know that approach to understanding the project they wish to discuss, and are unfamiliar with other ways of understanding it. Thus they insist that readers re-create their steps, inefficient and ineffective though they may be.

As a test, ask if your paper would have much more "punch" if some sections were cut out entirely. Peripheral subjects may not be easily identified as peripheral by the reader who does not know about the whole journey. They may decide the paper is not for them, or they may be disappointed because what they thought was a major focus is merely a stepping stone to other subjects.

There are other ways to sin, of course. At the other end of the continuum of reader frustration is the paper that begins speaking in midsubject, almost midsentence. The heart of the paper is there but the audience cannot see the total form; only fine-grain detail is provided. Once you stand back and see the problem, perhaps with the help of your writing community, the fix is obvious.

My more radical suggestion is to move the conclusion you have drafted to the beginning. The paper that sets up a tortuous path through many subjects typically hides its contribution. Almost always that paper does not highlight its own unique message until the end. I have already advised you to identify your contribution in the abstract. Consider the even more radical step of making the conclusion the introduction. You will have to follow with material you did not intend to put in the paper—but you may know what to write. If so, I'll bet that paper will be more interesting than the one you have been thinking about so far.

After considering these basic framing issues, give another thought to the busy reader. I hope you are still enthralled with the subject of the paper, but the reader can rarely be counted on to have the same enthusiasm. In fact, in a crowded world, any given message is unlikely to get much attention. Therefore ask yourself the following questions:

1. *Are the headings of my paper informative when read on their own?* You have a choice between headings that merely mark a subject ("Literature Review") and headings that provide more detail ("Conflicting Approaches to Understanding X"). Choosing the second will clearly give the skimming reader much more information; whether you choose it depends upon conventions in your field, but don't take convention as gospel.

2. *Can tables and figures be read without consulting the text?* Do they attract the reader? The skimming reader typically notices tables and figures because they stand out in the text. These too can be more or less informative. At the least, they should stand on their own, with basic information provided in a legend rather than in the text. As a set, they ideally highlight key findings and major points of the paper.

3. *Is the basic message of the paper clear from reading topic sentences?* The reader with some interest in the paper still may not read it entirely. I often move on to examine key sentences. These sentences must be clear and interesting to hold my attention.

4. *Do format, typeface, margins, and other typographical details make the paper easy to read?* Ultimately, the copy editor will be responsible for these issues; in the meantime, consider the reviewer. A good packaging job enhances a paper's content.

Conclusion

I have a hard time ignoring poor writing and incomplete logic in early drafts and tend to give authors unnecessary advice on style and other issues. You can focus the attention of your advice-giver on the issues that really need help if you establish the skeleton of your argument and ask for his or her response to this outline.

By the time you publish, it is important to hone this structure to clearly communicate your logic to the reader via clear headings, sub-headings, and topic sentences. Readers often outline the things they read with colored highlighters. If I can't do that easily, I often stop reading. It is a busy world. I don't have time to find the message that the author should have made apparent.

Chapter 8

⋰⋱

Introduction and Conclusion

The introduction is the first statement of any length in the conversation you have chosen. You must:

- *Show that you recognize the issues raised in past conversation*
- *Reinforce the language that characterizes your contribution*
- *Continue to demonstrate that you have something worthwhile to add to the conversation*

The conclusion should remind readers of your contribution; I suggest that it also add something new.

It is worth working hard on these important parts of the paper. Further, it is a good time to again ask for advice. This is the last point at which others can provide input easily.

Definition

The title and abstract of a written document initially attract readers; the *introduction* must strengthen their interest so that they will read on. It cannot reliably do so just by being unique or provocative. A good introduction must establish the direction and critical content of what follows.

It is useful to think of your reader posing a mental "test" on this opening conversational gambit:

- Is this work actually going to say something interesting to me?
- Will it be worth the effort to understand?

In the privacy of reading, pressed by many other things to do, most readers will overlook writing that doesn't quickly pass these tough tests.

Follow the Best Articles in Your Target Journal and Look to Conversants and Exemplars

Many people think of introductions as the hardest part of writing. I'm sure my description of a reader's test does not ease any anxiety you may have. However, you have several tough members of your audience at your side: your conversants. You can also look at your exemplar articles and the articles in your target journal for help.

Do a little research:

- How do they engage the reader's interest?
- How many citations do they use, if any?
- Do they give examples?
- How long are their introductions?
- How complex are their sentences?
- How do they balance general comments with specific information?
- How much background do they provide before moving into the topic of discussion?

Obviously, you can avoid the work of writing altogether if you get too involved with answering these questions, and procrastination definitely is to be guarded against. Still, taking time with others' introductions can get you into the rhythm of the conversation you are joining and the kind of contribution you want to make.

Then you must write your own.

EXERCISE 22

Draft the introduction to your paper.
Critique it yourself, then ask others for their advice.

Many people feel that the best way to begin writing is simply to begin. They work in free form for awhile, worrying as little as possible about starting at the right point. They may or may not try to be provocative. It's an expansive brainstorming mode; editing and focus come later.

If you have trouble knowing exactly what to write, it may be helpful to start by writing topic sentences. If you are really blocked, work on some other part of the paper. But be careful. I find that when I don't get the beginning more or less right, I have trouble later on; so circle back as quickly as possible and try again to write the introduction for your paper. (This advice is from my own experience; for an opposing perspective, read the conversation with Mary Jo Hatch in Appendix A.)

If brainstorming and evasion don't work, you might try a much more mechanical approach. Write a first sentence like the first sentence in one of your conversants' or exemplar papers. In fact, you can try just substituting your nouns for theirs. Often the result sounds remarkably apt, or at least reasonably intelligent. If so, work on the rest of the paragraph and/or paraphrase a few more sentences, then see if you can branch out on your own.

It can be very helpful to imagine yourself talking to people you know as you write this difficult part of the paper. I find that I speak more specifically if I have one person in mind, but I also have the following suggestion:

⸎ ⸎

Speak to a supportive, but somewhat skeptical (or distracted) friend.

⸎⸎⸎⸎

This image helps me start the conversation in the first paragraph. It focuses my attention on building a case for why my work is interesting, without making me defensive.

All this advice may not be helpful enough. The great problem with introductions is that so many different starting points are possible, and yet each one will make some difference in the order and tone of what follows. I often waste time proving this obvious point to myself. Thus it is also important to evoke the larger audience I am actually trying to attract. Thinking of conversation with the specific group of people I want to read my work has helped me decide on a starting point. In fact, I suggest a rather demanding test:

⋇ ⋇

If you can't naturally cite your conversants and several papers from your target journal in the first few paragraphs of your paper, rethink your target and/or your conversants.

⋇⋇⋇

Think in these terms even if the norms in your field or your target journal are for few citations in introductory material, and even if you plan to depart significantly from previous work. The test is whether you can employ ideas already in use to introduce and justify the importance of your own work. If you can't do this, the fault may be in the starting point you have chosen among many alternatives, or it may be a more basic mismatch among your chosen audience, outlet, and the work itself.

Critique the First Draft of Your Introduction Yourself

Once you are fairly comfortable with the basic material of your introduction, you can examine its structure more closely. Here is a summary of advice I frequently give:

1. Begin with the subject that truly interests you. As you edit your own work, and give advice to others, see if the introduction would be improved by cutting the first few pages of what you have written. I already offered this advice when discussing writing outlines but am amazed by how often major surgery continues to be a helpful move. Somehow it is hard to get to the heart of things. We need to warm up; maybe we feel we should "bow to the gods" that established the field. We want to move from general to specific. Remember conversation—you need to say something interesting, fast.

2. Be succinct. You might assume that introducing the topic of your paper would be easy enough. Often, however, an author's interest in a subject is frustratingly broad (and deep) in comparison with the aims of a specific paper. Typically, it is necessary to focus as well as decrease the amount of information offered. More colorfully, I have to remind myself to do the following:

❖ ❖

Curb "pack rat" tendencies.

❖❖

Pack rats are North American rodents that love shiny things. Their nests typically contain a mess of odd objects they've picked up over time: old gum wrappers, bottle caps, coins, and so on. I've had to admit that my scholarly interests have something of the same quality. They are broad and idiosyncratic enough to confuse the specific paper I am writing. This can be especially problematic in the introduction, where the reader is looking for clues about the main subject of a paper—my interesting aside can be easily misinterpreted as a major topic. Thus I have to repress my pack rat tendencies and present a more orderly, more easily understood account to my readers. The subject may demand complexity, and benefit from multiple perspectives, but I need to be disciplined about the subjects I introduce.

3. Make sure you provide some orienting background. Although I like papers that begin at a point of interest, I've already noted the problem of papers that seem to start in midsentence. In well-organized fields, with strong conversations established, this may be appropriate. You have to look to your conversants, and papers published in the outlet you have chosen, to determine how much orienting information is necessary. Don't forget to make this assessment, however, because what is obvious to you, working in the midst of your subject, will not be obvious to all readers.

4. Do not spend too much time on other people's work. I believe new writers in particular fall into the trap of saying too much about other people's work because their academic training has revolved around reading and reviewing the work of others. Think about having a real conversation with leaders in the field; you will certainly bore them if you spend much time talking about references they already know.

5. Make assertions about previous work that reflect your own judgment and agenda. You can make background material more useful if you move beyond description to make assertions that lead to your own study. "Work on X began in the early 1980s" is a relatively poor topic sentence, for example, when compared with "Work on X has provided relevant information on y and z in the last 20 years," especially if your contribution will tell us even more about x, y, and z.

6. Define key terms and new terms. Writers should not assume that their readers will define critical concepts in the way the writer defines them. Even a well-established topic frequently includes conflicting definitions and poorly understood concepts. If readers make assumptions you do not make (or vice versa), this can affect their interpretation of your work. Without going overboard or being too obvious, it thus is a good idea to be explicit about the exact way you are using key terms.

I feel strongly that, whenever possible, these should be terms that are used by other scholars. More specifically, I urge those in my class to:

＊ ＊

Avoid the temptation to coin new terms.

＊＊＊＊

Most people become scholars because they want to make their own unique contribution to a field. It's easy, however, to become too committed to a heroic "John Wayne" vision of doing everything yourself. Every new term makes communication with others more difficult; a proliferation of similar terms in a field confuses subsequent dialogue and retards scholarly progress. Thus you should try to avoid inventing words (good advice that I ignored when I introduced the term *conversants* in this book). If you can't find a way around using a new term, make sure it is succinctly defined.

7. Think about "voice." Look at your conversants and other recent work in your field to see if you are drawn to writing that clearly establishes the author's perspective. I respond to papers written in such a way that I can feel the authors' individual intelligence and point of view even when they do not use the first person pronoun, and I try to do the same. You will have to find a "voice" that works for you and is acceptable in your field. I do encourage you to avoid the voice of the "great all-powerful Wizard of Oz." That overauthoritarian tone is heard too often in scholarly writing. In their anxiety to sound confident, new authors in particular are drawn to this voice. It is not one that invites further conversation (which was the Wizard's intention).

8. Lay a "bread crumb trail" for the rest of the paper. All of this advice is about writing for an audience. I suggest you do one more thing as you work hard to make that connection. In the fairy tale, Hansel drops bread crumbs so that he and his sister can find their way though the forest. My suggestion is that you think about deliberately laying a similar trail for readers trying to find their way through your paper. In Chapter 6, I suggested that you identify three to five key words and use them in your abstract. These concepts should appear again in the introduction. The body of the paper should develop each idea, ideally in the order they appeared in the abstract and introduction. The conclusion should pick them up again. You help the reader if you mark the building blocks of your argument in this way.

Ask Others to Read Your Introduction

Although the theme is now well worn, I want to emphasize how important it is to ask for advice from others before working too long on your introduction. This is the last part of your paper that is relatively easy to ask others to read, because it is general and still relatively short. Once you begin working on the body of the paper, the manuscript is much longer, and to understand your work advisers need to know more about your field. You will be much more on your own, so get as much guidance as you can before you leave the introduction.

Advisers can help you focus on the most interesting aspects of what you have to say. They can help you cut asides and establish an agenda that can be carried out in the amount of space you are likely to be allowed. Don't be shy. Ask other people to read your introduction and keep working on it until you hear them say, "This is interesting!"

Write a Conclusion That Can Stand on Its Own

The classic advice given to students just learning to present or write is this: Tell the audience what you are going to say, say it, and tell them what you said. I think this advice is half right but misleading in scholarly settings.

Scholars have to be careful that they don't bore intelligent readers by repeating information from the introduction in the body of the paper and then reiterating it once again in the conclusion. The strategy of repetition also forfeits the opportunity to deliver as much information as possible to skimming readers, enticing them to read the whole paper because their time was well spent looking at a brief amount of material.

Alternatively, readers who have worked through the paper typically need to be pulled back to the big picture with a conclusion so they will remember the broadest possible application of your work. Skimming readers may not need the big framework, but they do need information about the contribution your work provides. Both kinds of readers deserve something new. Thus I encourage you to look ahead; add some last thought that enhances your work's significance.

I also encourage you to draft a conclusion before you write other parts of your paper. Not only will it provide another guidepost to keep you on track, it is a needed check to see if you can deliver enough content to join the conversation you hope to join. Do the following experiment.

EXERCISE 23

Before you finish your analysis and writing, draft the conclusion of your paper, going beyond what you are sure of to experiment with the most assertive statement of the paper's benefits that you can make.

I am not suggesting that you end up publishing a statement that lies about your accomplishments. When you have a final draft, you should make sure that the conclusion is accurate. But I have found that when people make a bold statement and are asked why they can't make it true, they often discover they can do more than they planned.

Conclusion

The introduction is an obviously important and visible part of your paper that is well worth attention. But if you always start at the introduction when you work on your paper, the introduction can become unnaturally muscle-bound. A former student of mine, Jung-Taik Oh, told me that there is a Korean saying that describes the problem perfectly: "Head of a dragon, tail of a cow." To minimize this imbalance, vary the points at which you start work on your paper. This is easiest to do if you are working with a strong outline.

It is particularly important to occasionally begin working on the end of your paper. You may find that writing a dazzling conclusion leads you to strengthen prior sections and again puts the paper in better balance.

Chapter 9

⋅⋚⋛⋅

Presentation

Presentation can be an intrinsic part of the research and writing process. Used deliberately, presentation:

- *Clarifies thinking about the subject of your work and thus subsequent writing*
- *Focuses attention on issues of communication, which will make it even more likely that the work will reach an audience*
- *Allows scholarly conversation to have an early input into the work itself*

I discuss it at this point in a book on writing because it is often a useful exercise before completing a formal contribution to scholarly conversation.

Definition

A *presentation* is a verbal account of one's work, delivered to a live audience.

Most of us resist or are afraid of public presentation, which may be why it is so helpful. As Samuel Johnson said in 1777 about the prospect of hanging in a fortnight, commitment to making a presentation "clarifies the mind wonderfully."[1]

Even those who are comfortable in front of an audience can benefit from trying to be more effective communicators. Just as thinking clarifies writing, writing also clarifies thinking, and presentation can clarify both. I often do not know whether the material I am writing is articulate or interesting—until I see blank or bored expressions on faces in the audience. That is very useful information; a fix before sending something out for review vastly improves its chances for publication. In other words, presentation adds a third useful component to the relationship between thinking and writing which I have been emphasizing all along (see Figure 9.1).

The contribution to thinking and writing is certainly a sufficient reason to pay attention to presentation and will be the dynamic emphasized here. The equally important reason to become involved with presentation, both as a speaker and as a member of the audience, is that the most exciting academic conversations typically take place at professional meetings and other face-to-face encounters. The presence of many scholars allows conversation to move quickly. People build on and refute each other's points, often coming to conclusions that no one had articulated before the conversation. It takes a long time to accomplish the same thing in written work. Even conversation on the Internet proceeds by fits and starts.

Furthermore, in live conversation, scholars interact from their current experience. Because it draws on work that has not yet been published, the participant in these conversations has a chance to leapfrog the conversation found in journals and other formal outlets of the field by several years. In the best of circumstances, your current thinking is changed for the better by the current thinking of the audience, making it more likely that those who ultimately read your written work will find it fresh and timely. Even a hostile audience (sometimes a hostile audience most of all, if you can maintain your capacity to listen) can provide a valuable critique of your logic.

The gain for the presenter thus far exceeds the pain of anticipating and delivering a live presentation. The act of preparing for a presentation involves the kind of organizing that will directly benefit writing. Good presenters ensure that their audience remembers their message; academic writers need to do the same. Even those who present easily are urged to seek these benefits, making sure that they leave the audience not only happy but informed.

Presentation Basics = Writing Basics

There are many different styles of presentation, just as there are many different styles of writing. Any type of presentation—lecture, informal discussion, even office conversation—can inform writing. The basics of verbal communication are the same basics you must consider in written presentation of your work. You must do the following:

- Capture the audience's attention
- Clearly identify your subject
- Provide an overview of the work that was done
- Make sure the audience understands your personal contribution to work that has been done in the past
- Leave them interested and wanting more

The relatively limited time one has in presentation intensifies the pressure to accomplish these basic tasks, which is why I often recommend that the people who work with me follow this advice:

❖ ❖

Try presenting before your first written draft.

❖❖❖❖

I've had good luck with this strategy. In fact, some of the things that I've found easiest to write followed the outline of presentation slides. When I talk in one- or two-day workshops about the material you are reading now, I use over 150 overheads. I reorganized and rewrote them several times. They were of enormous help when I decided I wanted to write a book. In this case, I decided I wanted to keep the "short message" style that comes from thinking in bullet points; for other kinds of writing, I follow the outline but move further from the tone of a presentation.

You may feel that you do not know enough to give a successful presentation until you finish writing, but up to a point this fear will make the exercise more valuable. Think of ways you can lower your discomfort. Can you give an illustrative example of the subject that interests you but that you have not yet researched in detail? Can you describe a case in which the process that interests you develops as you believe it should, or could? Can you organize the literature to date in a way that brings new insight to your field? It is hard to be more specific without knowing more about the work you are doing, but it should be clear that a successful presentation will probably call for new thought on your part, which is why it is a useful adjunct to writing.

My point is that presentation generates new challenges for the scholar. Scholarly communication has to have content—entertainment is not enough. Many of us who teach have had the unworthy thought born of envy that our most popular colleagues may be merely putting on a "good show." We have ourselves listened to delightful presentations that we could not later summarize. Yet we also have experienced presentations that were both insightful and involving, and naturally wish to do the same. Only the most dedicated scholar, already deeply immersed in an area of inquiry, will listen long to a poor presenter. A skillful presenter, on the other hand, reaches many who did not previously have an interest in her or his scholarship. This is the very goal that the scholar has in mind. Writing and presentation are thus allies, as shown in Figure 9.1.

It is very hard for me to know whether I am presenting the kind of detail scholarship demands in a presentation unless I write it down and examine it more closely. At the same time, often I do not know whether something I am writing is interesting or important until I see the faces of a live audience. I try to cut and augment what I am working on in response to this editorial advice. But this is not the only useful tension between writing and presenting. Presenting often brings a more immediate vocabulary and a fresher voice. It may require simplification, but it is often possible to convey a more complicated message in person. Each of these experiences can enrich the writing you are trying to bring to formal publication.

Early presentation is, of course, only one kind of presentation. As you complete your manuscript, and feel that you have done the very best that you can to develop your ideas in a compelling fashion, present again to test your confidence. If you are heading toward journal publication, this is basically a "pre-review." Interaction with a live audience allows you to anticipate and diffuse potential reviewer concerns, making publication more likely.

Presentation after publication also is an important part of disseminating your ideas. In a busy world, we all have more things we should read than we can read. Thus, even though the journal is on the shelf, or a manuscript has arrived in the mail, it does not mean that your work has actually been read. Despite your best efforts with the written word, you can use the opportunity to be more persuasive in person.

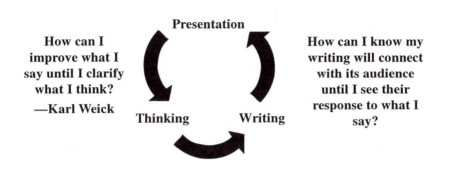

Figure 9.1. The Reciprocal Relationship Between Writing, Thinking, and Presentation

Although I have been telling you that presentation is of value to me because it organizes and simplifies my thoughts, my colleague Mary Jo Hatch uses presentation in a very different way. She finds that presentations are more fluid and less linear than writing, especially because she uses many diagrams and illustrations. She therefore prizes presentation as a way of exploring the complexity of what she ultimately wants to write about. She typically packs many more presentation slides than she can take advantage of, deciding on the day of presentation which she will use. Then, as Weick would suggest, she waits to "see what she will say" in response to these stimuli and audience interaction.

Obviously, you must seek your own benefits from presentation. The basic message of this chapter is that presentation is an important part of scholarly conversation, and perfecting multiple methods of conversing (especially presentation and writing but also e-mail and so on) facilitates successful scholarship.

Control Over Mechanics Increases the Gain From Presentation

You probably already know the basics of presentation. What interests me about the short list that follows is that it suggests a set of activities slightly different from those I typically urge on people who are writing, and yet each suggestion can improve writing.

1. Capture the attention of your audience. Almost always, the success of a presentation is established in the first few minutes of interaction. Important issues include the following:

- Speaker credibility, perhaps established by the person introducing you
- Eye contact, across the entire audience (many people favor one part of the room)
- Personal connection, easiest to establish by showing you care about and understand the audience

2. Focus audience attention on the main message of your presentation. It is often harder to deliver the message you intend to a listening audience than a reading audience. Control over the context, from lighting to time before lunch, helps capture audience attention. Overheads, handouts, notes on a board or flip chart are all visual pointers that can aid understanding, as are stories and questions to and from the audience. In each case, the device you hope will focus attention can go astray and be distracting, an issue that must be considered beforehand and monitored during the presentation itself.

3. Use visual aids if they fit the occasion. Acetate overheads or computer-aided presentations are a way of life in my field. I find them useful for keeping me, as well as the audience, on track. Once I have the basic pointers these tools provide, I may choose to abandon the outline, but it is my choice; the vagaries of the moment do not dictate the material I cover. There are a few rules for making these visual aids more effective:

- Number each slide (in case of accident and to easily reorganize your material after presentation).
- Use no more than one slide per minute of allocated presentation time.
- Use a limited number of words per overhead in *large* type.
- Use color if possible.
- Use diagrams, clip art, and other visual relief as appropriate.
- Use line-by-line building and other dynamic tools if available.
- Use pointers on more complicated slides.
- Continue eye contact with the audience, rather than looking at the machine or the screen.

4. Vary content and style to hold attention. Whatever methods you use to focus attention, it is important not to rely on just one device, even in a relatively short presentation. The alternatives depend upon the situation, but here are a few basics:

- Physically move around (but not excessively).
- Occasionally turn off the view-graph or computer, if you are using one (paradoxically, this can be an effective way of signaling an important point).
- Show a video clip, bring information from the World Wide Web, use a computer program to illustrate data dynamically.
- Ask the audience to do something (ask or answer a question, think about an issue in silence for a few moments, fill out a questionnaire).

5. Practice in the setting if possible. Last-minute snafus stymie effective presentation. Know where the light switches are, and how they work. If you're using electronic equipment, practice using it, and make sure it is effective from all points in the room. Know where replacement parts are located and have a backup plan if all electronics fail. Think about temperature, noise, and other distractions. Then, practice until you are comfortable with your material. People respond most easily to speakers who are at ease; they can give their attention to the message, not its bearer.

Take Time to Do It Right

If you are in the midst of writing, it is often hard to move to another activity, especially because gathering more facts or doing more analysis increases confidence. Unfortunately, many presenters invest too much time writing the paper that supports presentation, rather than organizing the presentation itself. It's a dysfunctional decision.

❧ ☙

Stop analyzing and writing in time to develop a good presentation.

❧❧

It is easier to follow this advice if you accept the basic thesis of this chapter—that presenting is a form of thinking and a way to refine thinking. It has its own logic and must be considered to be an activity that is distinct from writing, but it will improve writing. I recommend that you explore the benefits by planning a presentation from the paper that you have been preparing.

EXERCISE 24

Prepare a 10-minute presentation
in the format appropriate for a group you might
actually address. If at all feasible in this scenario,
prepare up to ten overhead slides with at least two
backups for discussion.

Formally present this work to others and ask
for their critique.

As you carried out this assignment, you probably found, as I typically do, that you know more about your subject than you thought. Perhaps you were able to describe parts of the project that you had been worrying over with less trouble than you anticipated. Further, you may have been congratulated for expertise that you did not realize you had, or for making innovative contributions that you had not valued so highly. At the same time, you probably found that you had to do more work to present some ideas than you expected, and certain arguments may have given you unexpected trouble as you talked to a live audience. Both the negative and the positive information you have gained will suggest new writing activities.

I hope the idea of "backup slides" was also useful. One of the most important decisions in preparing a presentation is the choice of what not to say. And yet, conversation during and after the presentation is often enriching because it explores new territory. Knowing what to say initially, what to reserve for later, and what to suppress altogether is one of the difficulties of writing. You were experimenting with possible solutions to that problem when you made backup slides.

Rehearse, Rehearse, Rehearse

This heading is not just a play on "location, location, location" (the three most important things about real estate investment). I want to draw your attention to different kinds of presentation preparation.

The first rehearsal involves imagining interaction with an audience, even before the presentation is organized. You have to "frame" a presentation in terms of an audience, just as you have to frame a written communication. It won't surprise you that I strongly believe it saves a lot of time to think about the norms of conversation before you begin. As discussed in Chapter 3, as well as in this chapter, the basic questions are these:

- Who am I talking to?
- What are their interests?
- What do they already know?
- What do I have to offer?
- How can I attract their attention?

A second important kind of rehearsal is done with oneself once the presentation is organized. I find it useful to stand up in front of a mirror, listening to and looking at myself presenting. Sometimes I start doing this before the presentation is complete. Even when I finish working on it, I try to rehearse by myself at least once, but usually many times, before I stand in front of an audience. In the process, I hone the message, give it more "punch," smooth complicated transitions, and so on.

A third kind of presentation rehearsal is made before one or more sympathetic friends. These may be members of your writing community who can tell you, in ways you are unlikely to be able to tell yourself, how your presentation comes across. They can discuss timing, delivery, posture, clothing, and so on, as well as critique content. Audio- and videotape can provide some of this information, but personal interaction is important. Ideally, you will have more than one person who can provide advice, but once again you must make sure that your inner compass is in good working order. You can't do everything. Don't let "helpful" critics lower your self-confidence.

Conclusion

Seek opportunities to present. No matter how good you are now, you can get better. Have someone videotape your performance. Although watching oneself can be even more painful than performing in front of a live audience, self-analysis of a video typically shows presenters that they are better than they feared they were and yet have things to work on that they had not worried about. Clubs, professional organizations, and other groups can provide you with additional advice. There also are many books, of varying utility, on presentation. The bibliography lists a few that Kurt Heppard and I have found helpful. Finally, it is important to critically examine successful presentations by others, gleaning ideas that will work in your professional settings.

Note

1. The full quote comes from Boswell's *Life of Johnson:* "Depend upon it, sir, when a man knows he is to be hanged in a fortnight, it concentrates his mind wonderfully" (*Bartlett's familiar quotations*, J. Kaplan, Gen. Ed., 16th ed., 1992, p. 317).

Chapter 10

⁖

Body of the Paper/First Full Draft

Given that I am deliberately trying to describe the generic process of writing, I can only be of limited help as you move into the hard work of conversing with a very specific academic audience. I do suggest that you:

- *Depend on conversants and other advisers in your field to help focus your arguments and highlight your accomplishments*
- *Pause again to analyze how you write most productively*
- *Use exemplars on other subjects to solve specific writing problems*
- *Edit with an eye for common pitfalls in academic writing*
- *Try to avoid putting aside partially finished manuscripts*
- *Work toward depth and complexity*

Rely on Conversants and Advisers in Your Field for Help With Content

You are now at the heart of the conversation you want to have, working with the material that interested you from the beginning. You have the advantage, but this is exactly where the hard work lies. A well-crafted title, abstract, and introduction can gain attention. Now you must deliver.

New and even more experienced authors sometimes fear that they do not have enough to say as they begin to discuss their material in depth. The first temptation may be to summarize what others have done. As already noted, this is not an interesting conversational gambit, although it may be a helpful warm-up. You must focus on what *you* are adding to the conversation. Every person has a unique perspective and unique experience. If you have gone through the work of identifying an interesting topic and have tried hard to develop new insights, you *do* have something to say. If you find that you need more material, you can cycle back to analysis.

You also must resist the fear that you won't be admitted to the conversation (which is somewhat different from worrying that you do not have enough to say). If you are not well known, remember that innovations and new insights often come from new voices in a discipline, and major journals do print work by unknown authors. Even if the particular effort you are working on now doesn't have the success you hope it does, practice is the only way you will become more adept at joining the conversation.

You should consult those who are already engaged in the conversation that interests you if you find getting started difficult. Ideally, you have advisers or mentors who can help you identify the most interesting material you have to offer and the strategy you might follow in presenting it. Whether or not you can engage in live conversation on these issues, your conversant papers/books are a useful source of help. I encourage people who work with me to consult these sources in the following way:

EXERCISE 25

Carefully read each of your conversant works.
Write as many comments in the margins as possible, striving
to match every detail of their work with details from
your own thinking and research.

Once pressed to say something about *each* aspect of a conversant's work, people who carry out this exercise typically find they have more to write about than they realized. Not all of their marginal comments will fit in the paper they are currently drafting, but they have a large stockpile of ideas with which to begin.

In fact, once you get started writing the body of your paper, you may well find that you have too many ideas and that they lead you in too many different directions. Although I admire papers that are dense, provoking thoughts that I did not have before mentally conversing with the author by reading his or her paper, divergent thoughts are "red herrings." Like the smelly fish pulled across the trail to divert hounds in a fox hunt, an interesting aside distracts readers from the major points a paper is trying to make. Informal and formal responses to the writing workshops I have given indicate that my advice for dealing with this problem is one of the most useful suggestions I make:

Keep a "dump" at the end of your computer file for material that must be pruned.

A dump will help focus your attention on the *one* paper you are writing now. You will occasionally resurrect something for the paper you are currently writing, and you are creating a "gene pool" for future writing.

Sooner or later, however, you may encounter something that feels exactly like the "writer's block" of fiction writers. In fact, most authors find that they sometimes have difficulty maintaining momentum. A practical tip for overcoming this common writing problem comes from Ernest Hemingway:[1]

Always leave something easy to write as a warm-up task for the next day.

In the end, patience and time are essential as you shape your paper; there is no reason to assume that writing about complicated subjects of scholarship will be easy. But whether it goes smoothly or is difficult, you must write. Try to do it every day. Anne Lamott[2] and many others suggest that you write as daily exercise. If you are stuck, you can work on the more mechanical aspects of your paper. Draw charts, fix tables, check the bibliography; these may lead you to more difficult work.

On the other hand, this structured approach may break down entirely. Mary Jo Hatch, in the conversation recorded in Appendix A, says she often starts by writing in a journal. She identifies the overall subject of a given paper long after she begins working on the core. If this method seems as if it might work, start there. Just write.

Write, that is, until you have to admit that you really are not making progress. When I was trying to finish my dissertation, I twirled my family around for an entire summer. I was determined to have it completed before my new job began in the fall. Yet I was making more trouble for myself with each day at my desk. Finally I put the manuscript aside, we moved, and in three weeks I wrote what I couldn't write in three months. It would have been better, not only for the writing but for life in general, to have taken a break much earlier.

Go to Exemplars for Formatting and Stylistic Help

The exemplars you have collected should continue to be useful guides as you work on the heart of your paper. Look at the number of pages devoted to different topics, the level of detail, the way transitions from topic to topic are carried out, the way examples are used, how data are presented. Also, do not be afraid to consider content. If an exemplar writes about five contributions of their work, for example, when you have only identified two of your own, you will almost certainly be able to think of a few more if you analyze the different kinds of contributions your successful exemplar claims.

Pay particular attention to how exemplars keep the reader's attention. A clear and consistent "story line" or bread crumb trail is one of the hardest things to achieve in complicated scholarly writing, and the thread is typically lost in the middle of the paper. If you feel your subject matter is losing focus, examine your exemplars. See if you can use the devices that they use to more clearly center the topic you are writing about. As noted in Chapter 5, you may be forced to find additional exemplars if this or other problems you face are not well covered by the specific exemplars you have chosen. It may be especially useful to gain insight by going to the journal you hope will publish your work.

Commit to Writing a First Draft
in a Short Period of Time

Many successful academics write to tight deadlines, often accepting writing or speaking engagements before a draft is finished. If you do not have such a deadline in your immediate future, I suggest you make one up.

EXERCISE 26

Prepare a complete draft of your paper over the next three weeks, then take a week to edit your efforts.

The logic of this exercise is as follows. First, a relatively quick deadline seems to work for most people. We often waste time mulling over a paper, trying different approaches, waiting for inspiration. Yet, as the comic strip character Calvin once explained to Hobbes, the inspiration to write often comes from sheer panic. A few weeks is not much time until you must "go public"; as this raises your activity level, you will push other obligations aside. So be it. In my experience, writing requires significant blocks of time and they are always stolen from other demands.

Once a commitment is made, writing often takes on its own momentum. When I am really engaged by a writing project, I can work on it at the kitchen table, in a coffeehouse, in the car, almost anywhere, even when surrounded by relative chaos. I try to nourish the mood as long as possible because I know that I am getting two or three times as much work done as I normally would. The phrase to keep in mind:

When a writing project is hot, keep working!

In addition to the pleasure of momentum, there are several other reasons to push for a "complete" draft as early as possible. First, it is possible that writing will bring to light a significant deficiency in your logic, data, or analysis that requires rethinking the project, or at least its timing. It's better to know this as quickly as possible, before spending more time on a framework that cannot reach your intended audience in its current form.

Another reason to quickly draft your paper is that it will help balance subsequent efforts. Once I have a "complete" draft, it is easy to skip from one part of the paper to another, out of sequence, as energy and time are available. I can efficiently be unstructured, and often find I am interested in working on parts of the paper out of sequence. Before this point, I waste time on topics and approaches that will not fit and are ultimately dropped.

This is also the time to correct the "head of a dragon-tail of a cow" phenomenon. Even when I try to outline in even proportions, it is sometimes hard to make the heart of my paper as dense as the works I admire most. I often find it energizing to go back to the literature, using my conversants' bibliographies as a start. This is where the conversation metaphor comes into its own: Good conversation volleys back and forth, following one expected response with another less expected, developing one insight after another. The papers I admire take me along, making some surprising turns, to reach insights I hadn't considered before.

I will admit to being a bit too Pollyannaish[3] here. When I go back to the literature, I am sometimes frozen in place. I often find several articles I could have written, but didn't. Sometimes they suggest that the message I've been trying to frame is not as interesting as I once thought. I try to copy these disturbing articles, and then take a break. With a little time and a broader view, I can usually reframe what I've been trying to say. Although it's a scary experience, the result is what I'd hoped for: a more complex contribution to the literature.

At other times, going back to the literature is not at all helpful. To move along the accordion path of scholarship, I have to stand back. Unique contributions to the literature require something new; I have to find that within myself, within my data, from observing phenomena that have nothing to do with my subject. To find something new, I sometimes abandon not only the literature but the draft at hand, open a new computer file, and try to get a fresh start.

Be Alert to the Many Forms of Plagiarism and Dishonesty

Blank pages in the heart of a paper make everyone nervous. I assume, because you are reading a book on writing, that you are serious and careful about your work. It probably is not necessary to say that the two greatest scholarly sins are, first, to fabricate data or report work that was not done and, second, to claim work that is not your own. Although it may be tempting to fill the void in these ways, if you are found out, the consequences can (and should) be very serious.

Beyond the obvious, however, are more shadowy issues. For example, some people do not realize that "self-plagiarism" is possible. Reporting the "same" work under different titles to somewhat different audiences is problematic, although norms differ from field to field. When you go to conferences, be careful that you are presenting work that has not been heard by this audience before. Even more important, once you have published something, you must treat it as part of the public domain. If you publish the same words again, without sufficient citation, you are plagiarizing.

There are also gray areas in claiming the work of others. As you read the literature, you will absorb other authors' opinions. Even their vocabulary can become wedded to your own. It is fairly easy to repeat these ideas without citation, or to summarize a body of literature in a way that is less your opinion than the opinion of others who have surveyed the same terrain. I went to a college that took a strong stand on these issues, and I ended up feeling that the only safe course was not to read at all! Please don't go that far, but remember that opinion and point of view, even more than a specific string of words, deserve credit.

Keep thinking about conversation. When talking face-to-face, most people are careful to say, "I agree with what you said the other day," before they repeat something they heard. Similarly, we rarely say something in an ongoing conversation as if it just occurred to us if we have already made the point before. In both cases, recapitulation is almost always just a starting point. We repeat ourselves or others to make further arguments, which is how the center of your paper will gradually take shape.

Learn From Your Writing Experience

The ability to step back from the minutiae of daily writing to consider the project as a whole is critical. After finishing a full draft, I suggest you stop for more formal assessment.

EXERCISE 27

Reanalyze your writing habits and your writing strengths and weaknesses so that you can speed and improve subsequent writing.

Write down the times and location of your writing efforts over the last three weeks. What days, and time of day, were you able to write, given your other commitments? Would other times be more productive? Where did you do your best writing? What helped inspire good writing? What helped you move beyond the blocks that are inevitably encountered in writing? Such insights, put into action, will speed the completion of this and subsequent writing projects.

In addition to thinking about process, critique the content of this draft to understand more about your strengths and weaknesses as a writer. Drawing on this and other writing experiences, identify the kind of writing you do most easily. It is tempting to focus on the things you do best; ask yourself whether you put too much of this material in your work. Think of strategies to identify and support the parts of the paper that are the weakest, going back to conversants, exemplars, and human advisers as appropriate.

Edit to Avoid Common Problems

Examination of my own work, and the work of others, suggests that early drafts often err in some predictable ways. One piece of advice I give fairly often, for example, has to do with the way methodological weaknesses are discussed. Frequently authors overapologize. Worse, they often undercut their contribution by pointing out inevitable weaknesses at the end of the paper, potentially leaving the reader with a diminished opinion of the work that has been accomplished. All methodologies have strengths and weakness. (A good overview can be found in McGrath's discussion of "dilemmatics."[4]) As an author, it is very useful to remember that your reader is probably familiar with these issues. The average reader knows, for example, that it is hard to generalize from small sample studies. In many cases, it is not necessary to belabor the obvious.

Another common problem can be avoided by reminding the reader of critical information in the later stages of a paper. I am aggravated when I have to search back to find initial hypotheses so that I can understand results, for example. In a case study, it is often frustrating to be expected to remember the roles of key players or key dates. Understanding quantitative results shouldn't require remembering obscure variable abbreviations. Remember too that not all readers will proceed systematically through your paper; your results will gain more attention and understanding if they can stand alone.

I also urge you to make sure you have discussed the implications of your work for other subjects and future scholarship in your own area. Many authors appear to feel that the importance of their work is obvious. You should remember that readers do not have your detailed knowledge. Left on their own, they may draw less impressive conclusions than you would like them to. Rise above description! Comment on a broader scale, linking your work to the work of others.

On the other hand, some writers claim too much when discussing the contributions of their work, angering readers familiar with the literature by ignoring similar work done by others. (A particularly peeved reviewer will obviously be the person who has done some of that work.) My advice is to reexamine the overall conversation to remind yourself what you bring to the table. And look again at exemplars to find graceful ways of making those contributions obvious to readers.

Think About Order, and Disorder, as You Write

Scholars have an obligation to improve the reader's understanding of the subjects they study. This is a matter of insight, but insight is aided by logical presentation, and signaling. Thus, in Chapter 6, my advice was to make the order of the abstract reflect the order of the paper. This is an important device to establish an orderly framework that will orient the reader. Heading structure is a second; topic sentences are a third. Especially as the work gets complicated, the logic carried by these markers becomes more and more important. The more logical the writing, the more the reader can absorb.

To have a real impact, however, you must also help readers see new things that they have not noticed. Logic can be the enemy in this task because it lures the writer as well as the readers down familiar paths that do not require new thought. Make sure that you have not been writing on "automatic pilot"—reiterating arguments and conclusions you may not even agree with. A break in expectations is required. As you present your work, make unexpected turns that lead to and reinforce new insights. Stylistically, this may mean being evocative, or provocative, rather than logical.

In my opinion, excellent scholarship is marked by successfully mastering the difficult dual agenda of being clear, and challenging what is too clear. Once again, I urge you to ask for help as you try to find the balance.

EXERCISE 28

Find several peers with whom to exchange first drafts. Provide each other with written comments focused on overall structure and message.

As the recipient of advice, decide how you will revise your paper, discussing your revision plan with someone who was not part of the review process, if possible.

An outside overview is the objective of advice given at this point, although smaller observations on writing style, format, and so on also can be helpful. You might look again at the norms for advice-giving found in Chapter 1 to make the exchange supportive. Then, look in Appendix C for some guidance on the content of a helpful review. Separate the person from the work, and help yourself and your colleague make significant improvements in the next draft.

This exercise suggests that you get advice from multiple sources, which helps you see the range of possible responses to your work. But disparate and conflicting advice almost inevitably results and can easily be confusing. Your internal compass is the first defense. Discussion with others not involved in the reviewing process is a second aid to develop distance from the review, and thus your own perspective on the work at hand.

I also suggest that you exchange first drafts among peers. In general, this is not the point to deplete the limited stock of goodwill in those whose advice you may need later in the process, and you should be careful about the impression you make on people whose opinion may be important to you. If you can find others who are at the same stage in the writing process, the burden of reading a full draft can be balanced by reciprocity, and you have the opportunity both to take a break from your own paper and perhaps to bring back insight from considering someone else's issues.

Don't worry too much that the inexperienced are trying to lead the inexperienced. We all know more than we know how to execute in our own work. Revisiting Karl Weick's aphorism, sometimes we find out what we know by seeing how we advise others.

I often become too focused on a writing project; giving as well as getting advice restores balance. If the advice is not good, the very act of reasserting my direction can be helpful. But I also have to be careful of rejecting advice too quickly. I have repeatedly found that I hold on to certain aspects of my paper, despite advice, only to ultimately decide that the editorial suggestion was a good one.

Conclusion

When our daughter was about 3, she learned to be afraid of the dark from the TV program *Sesame Street*. As Grover began to repeatedly comfort her that "there really are not any monsters under the bed," she began to worry, needing reassurance and a night-light she had not needed before. This chapter's discussion of various writing blocks may perform the same disservice. If you have never experienced the difficulties I discussed in this chapter, I hope you skimmed by and will similarly ignore "helpful" passages in other books on writing.

My purpose is to contribute to your forward progress. Perhaps the most common review letter I receive as an editor says, in one way or another, "The authors had a great idea, but do not carry through on their promises." This chapter in particular is written to help you avoid such criticism.

Unkept promises are also a problem for manuscripts that reviewers never see. Most writers have files of partially finished drafts. I feel that I have too many of them myself. In some cases, I genuinely lost direction. Writing, or review, made it clear that I did not sufficiently understand my subject, or did not have enough to say. I try to file such projects neatly away, in the hope that I'll be able to make use of the time I've spent at some point in the future.

In many other cases, I was sidetracked by other obligations: the beginning of the teaching term, a holiday, a presentation I promised. When the rest of life gets in the way, a manuscript can turn as cold as it does from lack of confidence or a negative review. Even if the draft is fairly far along, it's hard to pick it up and decide what to do next. More important, over time I lose the enthusiasm that sustained writing requires. This is a regrettable loss of effort and thought.

Thus I urge you to manage your time to minimize incomplete writing projects. Scholarship is frustrated by not coming to publication. Keep writing!

Notes

1. Hemingway, E. (1984). *Hemingway on writing* (L. W. Phillips, Ed.). New York: Scribner, pp. 41-42.
2. Lamott, A. (1994). *Bird by bird*. New York: Pantheon.
3. Porter, E. (1977). *Pollyanna*. Laurel, NY: Lightyear. (Original work published 1913)
4. McGrath, J. (1982). Dilemmatics: The study of research choices and dilemmas. In J. E. McGrath, J. Martin, & R. A. Kilka, *Judgment calls in research*. Beverly Hills, CA: Sage.

Chapter 11

⁙

Revision, Submission, Revision, and Publication

As with almost everything else in life, a writing project often takes longer to complete than expected. It is hard to know whether the time is necessary or the result of doubt and indecision. This final chapter therefore offers advice in opposites:

- *Expect to revise, and then revise some more before submitting your work for publication, but do not hold on to it for too long.*
- *Once the paper has been submitted and reviewed, seriously consider recommendations for change, but do not feel you have to carry out all suggestions offered.*
- *Stick with your initial publication target, but move to other outlets if necessary.*

Revision Is a Critical Aspect of Scholarship

Almost every time you work on your paper, I believe that you should read and consider the current appropriateness of the following:

- Title
- Abstract
- Outline
- Headings
- Introduction
- Project description
- Analysis of data

- Interpretation of findings
- Contributions claimed, etc.

The first task of revision is to recheck the content of each element of your paper. The checklist found in Appendix C can help you make sure that you have not missed things that reviewers are likely to look for. Similar lists from journals or professional associations in your field can also be extremely helpful.

The second task of revision involves style. Go back to the basic writing rules summarized in Chapter 6 and make a separate pass through the manuscript to work on each piece of advice. Can you shorten any sentences? Do you repeat yourself? If so, be your own editor and cut without mercy. It's amazing to me that I often need to do that but then find paragraphs in which each sentence should be expanded into a paragraph of its own to clarify my argument.

After you've worked on these difficult "airtime" issues, go back again and consider grammar. Do you use present tense and active voice? Are your constructions unduly complicated? Then look at word choices: Do you find that you've overworked the same nouns and verbs? Luckily, most word processors have a built-in thesaurus. Be careful, however, about changing the words you use for key concepts; readers may wonder whether you are (or should be) talking about a second idea. A grammar check program may alert you to other problems. Sometimes the advice of the one attached to my word processor is absolutely nonsensical, but I also have learned that I systematically make errors that would horrify my seventh-grade English teacher. Most authorities are less rigid these days; I therefore ignore some advice, even in a book on writing. For example, I may interpose an adjective because I want to emphasize that you should *quickly* do something rather than *do something* quickly.

But each of these decisions is risky. The trade-off is between using a voice that feels comfortable and relevant but one that may distract some readers into thoughts about their grammatical training and opinions. It's particularly tricky for writers whose first language is not English. Appendix B records a conversation with Jone Pearce in which we both urge scholars to avoid homogenizing their work to the point of diminishing their own unique perspective. As reviewers and readers, we can help by not insisting on rigid rules that distance and tame scholarship. As authors, we can edit egregious mistakes so that the conversation about grammar will be about intentional emphasis, not what we were too tired to polish.

As you work, I encourage you to look at the classic reference book *The Elements of Style*[1] to make your decisions. The bibliography also praises *The Gregg Reference Manual*,[2] which goes into greater detail and is somewhat easier to use. Connie Luoto, who proofread this manuscript, actually loves reading this manual. I'm less enthralled by any grammar book but am trying to internalize the rules of grammar so that I can naturally write in ways that will not need extensive editing later.

Finally, read your paper and listen with an inner ear. Can you hear yourself speaking, or is the tone too stilted or remote for your taste? If you capture the tone you would like to achieve in some places, is it lost in others? Are some words too pedantic while others are too informal? I go over my work again and again, making small changes in an effort to achieve a consistent and engaging point of view. Of course, I don't always succeed, but I do believe that the time is well spent. In fact, this is one of several points that Mary Jo Hatch and I agree on in Appendix A, even though we have very different approaches to the writing task.

The point is that no one I know can write a perfect first draft; many of us write very imperfect ones. The good news is that once something is on paper (or in the computer), it can be reorganized, pruned, expanded, and clarified. If you want to maximize your chances for publication, you have to have patience with this process of refinement.

Keep reading the things you write, word for word; don't just block and move. Word processors and fast printers make it easy to ignore large chunks of one's work. In fact, you should expect changes in every aspect of what you are working on, right up to the point of submission, as your thinking about the work improves. New authors are often astounded by how many drafts lie behind a piece of work they admire. The number depends upon circumstance and author, but dozens of drafts are not unusual for considered scholarship.

You will not get the full benefits of redrafting, however, if you do not work with the manuscript as a whole. Soon after I have a "complete" draft in hand, I start working on paper, rather than on the computer, because I can see the whole so much more clearly. I always cut and add rather large passages; I always reanalyze whole sections of the paper. It is worth reiterating:

꙳ ꙳

Don't fall in love with anything you have written.
Be willing to cut, revise, and reorganize every word
of every draft.

꙳꙳꙳꙳

On the other hand, know when to stop the introspective process of revision, because it is also possible to revise too much. In a class that lasts for a semester, I don't let revision go on for more than a week or two because I want a second draft in time to ask others for advice again before actual submission.

EXERCISE 29

Prepare a second draft to exchange for review,
making sure that it is a complete draft with all
tables, figures, and bibliography.

Prepare a formal written review of the papers you
receive for review.

Make a formal response to the reviews you receive
as author, then redraft your paper.

It is a good change of pace, after completely revising a paper, to consider two or three other people's work at the same stage. Don't forget the checklist found in Appendix C as a helpful guide. When working on the details of someone else's draft, I again often find that I get new insights into my own paper's weaknesses and strengths.

Further, it is very useful to have several different perspectives on my own work before formal submission. Multiple comments provide a more well-rounded review, and advice for change is more likely to be taken when in stereo. As already noted, it is very hard to get this kind of time-consuming attention from others, especially at the same point in time. A class exercise, or an agreement in a writing community, is by far the most likely source of multiple reviewers for a full draft. (Although this is a very good time to ask for advice from a dissertation adviser or other published mentor.)

The idea of an accordion path continues to be helpful to me as I pace this kind of input. I start redrafting by looking for new and better ideas in response to my own reading of a "final" draft, experimenting without being too judgmental, before going back into the mode of self-critique. Then I ask others for criticism. Depending on the advice, and my response, I may move back into an expansive phase of new input several more times.

Submit!

Once in the cycle of review and revision, you obviously are moving toward formal submission of your paper for publication. How close you are depends upon your own sense of the paper, taking into account the opinions you receive from others. In addition to the distribution of your paper for formal comments, this is a good point to present the paper, as recommended in Chapter 9. It also is a good point to review recent literature that you may have missed in the consuming process of research and writing. Not only are new contributions to academic conversations being made all the time, you are likely to see new points of contact between your work and the work of others now that your thinking has been further clarified by working with a complete manuscript.

Do not skip these steps, even if you must work alone. The following advice makes the point more explicitly:

Never submit an unfinished work
"just to see the comments."

Scholars who are new to a field sometimes think that it will be worth sending a relatively "uncooked" paper for conference or journal review just to receive comments. *Don't do it!* Because the paper does not represent what you know you can do, the advice you get is likely to be the kind of advice you could give yourself. Further, you cannot afford to get a reputation for being a shallow or disorganized thinker. (Blind review is some protection, but the editor does know who you are, and his or her opinion is very important.) Worse yet, something you are not very proud of could get published. As a permanent part of your vita, it could be the basis of decisions you may not even know are made. Don't risk it.

Once you are relatively happy with content, try to find a last bit of energy for polishing. After many drafts, a "final" version typically contains incomplete or inaccurate references, spelling errors, and mis-numbered or missing tables. Too often this is the version that goes out for review. An editor looking at an early copy of this book thought I did not give enough emphasis to the importance of careful editing before submission. Her concern is an important one: "As reviewers read through such a paper, they come to mistrust the author's scholarship, thinking that a sloppy paper reflects sloppy thinking." That's definitely worth thinking about.

On the other hand, don't fall into perpetual revision, holding on to your paper until the opportune moment for joining a conversation passes. Decide, with the help of those who know you, whether you tend to err on the side of submission too early or too late, and take appropri-ate action.

More experienced scholars under pressure are also tempted to submit early drafts because they run out of time for redrafting. Again my tendency is to counsel, "Don't do it," for the reasons just given. But I withhold that advice. Many experienced authors do well with rela-tively early submission because they are in control of the basics. Let your internal compass be your guide.

EXERCISE 30

Submit your paper, exactly following all submission
guidelines, with a brief cover letter.

The instruction to follow guidelines is an especially important part of this exercise, which is the last in the book. The rules of submission are often long and tedious. The bureaucratic feel of these guidelines can be annoying. Tight deadlines can lead you to pay insufficient attention to specifics. The paper that falls short of submission requests may still be put through the review process, although you risk additional delay if it is returned. Whether or not you skate by, you have almost certainly aggravated an editor and/or editor's assistant by not following his or her procedures. They are too important to your future to be irked by your inattention.

Finally, be content with a short letter of transmission. If you feel the editor needs instruction about the background or purpose of the paper, put such signposts in the paper itself. The busy reader is less motivated than the editor to classify your work. If a short letter is all you need, you can be more confident that the paper includes the information readers need.

Reviewer Comments Can Be Derailing

There is a wonderful elation in submission, which should be enjoyed to the fullest.

ᛜ   ᛜ

Celebrate submission as a victory in itself.
Take time off; tidy your desk.

ᛜᛜ

I find that keeping my enthusiasm for writing depends upon breaking up the writing process. Writing distracts me from other obligations; I need periodic housekeeping. There are disappointments along the way; I have to regroup. There are also many opportunities for satisfaction. Submission is certainly one of the most important. It deserves a night out, and more.

Unfortunately, the pleasure of getting a major project off one's desk is almost always followed by nervous anticipation of the reviewers' opinions about that work. Even if you can resist dysfunctional behavior during the wait, few experiences equal the hopeful/nervous moment when the envelope from the editor actually arrives.

If the news is good, congratulations on a job well done! You have found a way to contribute to scholarly conversation.

If the news is not good, do not lose heart:

- Give yourself some time (it takes me at least a week to be able to read a negative review thoroughly).
- Go over the advice offered several times.
- Make a photocopy so that you can make notes in the margin on how you might respond.
- Seek the opinion of others, including those who reviewed your manuscript before submission.
- Decide which suggested actions fit the contribution you want to make, and why you do not feel other suggestions are appropriate.
- Write a formal response to each specific comment, paying particular attention to your rationale for not following any advice given.
- Draft a cover letter thanking the editor and reviewer for their time and contributions to your work.
- Make appropriate changes in the paper itself.

This compendium definitely reflects North American conventions, which Jone Pearce and I critique in Appendix B, but you need to converse with your reviewers and to use that conversation to further improve your own thinking. If you have been invited to revise and resubmit, you now have the material in hand. Even if your submission was rejected, written response to reviewers and appropriate changes in the text itself are a useful device for further clarifying your purpose and justifying your arguments.

Please, do not ignore negative reviews. And do not overreact. In the worst-case scenario, an author decides to stop work altogether on a criticized project. Even the author who drops the portion of a paper that a reviewer questions, without agreeing that the paper is better off, is not participating in academic conversation as an equal.

Remember that even the most conscientious reviewer has only spent a few hours on a paper that you have spent much more time considering.

Reviewers' opinions have to be taken into account; their fresh perspective is critical for understanding what you are and are not communicating successfully. But they cannot know as much about what you have done and are trying to communicate as you do. The voice of reviewing often sounds more authoritative than it should, given these realities.

Also, remember that your work will inevitably evoke a range of reactions. The reviewers responding to your paper are only two or three data points from a much larger set, and neither you nor the editor can be sure where they fall in the population of future readers.

In short, an internal compass is critical for responding to review. You want to be strong enough to listen to and profit from the advice of those who have taken the time to read your arguments in their entirety. They have given your work far more time and attention than the average reader will give it, and thus their opinions are valuable. You are almost certainly well advised to follow their suggestions and make some painful decisions about cutting and changing what you have written.

However, writers often feel demeaned by the review process. In their eagerness for publication, they try to rewrite to order, but the work no longer feels like their own. I can think of a few cases where this behavior appeared to be necessary to gain the publication desired, but I strongly believe these cases are limited in number.

Rather than reluctantly following advice you do not agree with, treat the review process itself as part of the conversation of scholarship. I've had good luck presenting an argument to an editor about why I did not feel one or two suggestions fit my paper. Write to the editor and reviewers if, upon careful consideration, you do not agree with some of the advice you have been given. Indicate that you have heard and understand their point of view. Almost always this is not just a letter-writing task. Your arguments should appear in the paper itself; they will help convince other readers who might respond the same way reviewers did.

Find Another Outlet If Necessary

If you followed my earlier suggestions, you already have a backup journal in mind for a rejected paper. However, I believe you have work to do before putting the paper into the mail again.

❖ ❖

Never resubmit without redrafting.

❖❖❖❖

There are three reasons that I feel strongly about this advice. First, every outlet has its own history of conversation and its own personality: To maximize your chances of getting into the conversation, you have to reflect that unique setting. Sit down and read through past issues of your new target journal. Imagine yourself talking with these people on the subjects they have been addressing in this forum. The introduction, the way you frame your paper, the details you offer, the discussion of your work's significance are all likely to change subtly from your last draft because you are now trying to enter a somewhat different conversation. (You might remember that one important sign that you are in true conversational mode is that you can naturally cite previous work from your new target in your paper.)

The second important reason to revise before resubmission is that you may get reviewers similar enough to one or more of your first reviewers that they have similar concerns about your manuscript. You are much more likely to convince them to accept your work if you have redrafted your paper and addressed these issues. You certainly don't want to risk a second rejection on the very grounds that led to your first disappointing response.

Third, the odds are fairly high that your work will be sent to one of the very reviewers who has already seen your work. I find it annoying to be asked to spend time on a manuscript that has already received my attention if the author has not seriously considered my original comments. It is not that I expect every bit of my advice to be followed, especially for a different outlet, but my frustration with not being taken seriously is likely to color my second response. As an editor, I also respond negatively when I find that an author has not paid attention to the results of the last submission. These authors act as if publication were a mindless game of chance. That is certainly not my definition of scholarship. Be proactive; turn on your computer and improve your paper before putting it back in the mail.

Conclusion

This book is based on the idea that publication is a critical mode of scholarly conversation that lies at the heart of every discipline. Nothing that I have talked about is more likely to lead to publication than a commitment to revision, and resubmission. It surprises me that many people fall by the wayside just as they reach these final phases of the writing process. I think this is because they realize that after all the work that they have done, there is still considerable work to do before publication success.

Too often new scholars in a field also lose their idealism at this point and begin to characterize their field as elitist, conservative, and unable to recognize new voices and approaches. These are legitimate problems of academia. If you have some concerns along these lines, I hope you continue to hold them as you become more active in your field and can do something about them.

Because you *can* push through to publication and participation. Although the problems just noted are often real, the processes leading to publication also have some helpful and worthwhile features that are hard to see the first few times around. Once you begin to review, for example, it is easier to understand some of the thinking behind suggestions that initially seem arbitrary or unnecessary.

Further, with observation and analysis, it is possible to seek out conversations that are more likely to be welcoming. You will be able to formulate projects in which your training, background, and interests make you more likely to succeed. You can find colleagues who are interested in forming a supportive writing community that will increase the odds of achieving publication within a reasonable period of time.

But I will insist in closing that it is not just the brass ring of publication that you are trying to catch. Careful thought about the process of writing, and having fun with others engaged in the same process, can make work with a manuscript that is never published a valuable experience. You may gain only clearer, more complex, more interesting thoughts by trying to publish the paper you are working on now. But is that not the true goal of scholarship?

Notes

1. Strunk, W. (1972). *The elements of style, 2nd edition.* New York: Macmillan.

2. Sabin, W. A. (1992). *The Gregg reference manual* (7th ed.). New York: Glencoe/McGraw-Hill.

Appendix A

❖

A Contrarian Conversation
With Mary Jo Hatch

As I began to hold workshops on writing at Cranfield University, I found from several interesting conversations that my colleague Mary Jo Hatch's successful writing followed few of my prescriptives. She agreed to present an alternative view at the next workshop I held. The transcript below is our joint reconstruction of that session.

A: *Jo, thanks a lot for coming today. My purpose is to end today's session by asking you to provide a counterpoint to the writing methods we've just covered. I admire your writing tremendously; it is energized, theoretic, and often makes me think in a new way. From talking with you, I know that your approach to writing is very different from mine. Will you please tell us what you do?*

MJ: Let me start by saying that if you can follow the advice that you've gotten today, you should. It's probably the most straightforward way of getting to publication, and if you can do it, I congratulate you. But I can't do it. It's not the way I write.

I think my problem with Anne's model stems from my early training in English literature and journalism. I spent a difficult period trying to reconcile that beginning with my academic life. Outlines didn't and don't work for me. I never responded well to set assignments in class. They got in the way. I was much more creative if what I was working on felt like an essay or, better yet, like exploration.

What works for me is to begin by writing a whole lot of two- or three-pagers. It's not efficient. I write every day. I begin early in the morning, usually starting by at least 6 o'clock, and write two to

129

four hours. I'm writing to find out what I think; there's no agenda (well, these days there usually is, but while I developed my writing style this was my typical approach, and I still prefer it and do unsolicited papers this way). I just get thoughts, random thoughts, down on paper. After some time, the pages I am producing begin to have some coherence and that is when I start writing toward a first draft. Oddly, I rarely read those early two or three pages, though I keep them for quite a long time just in case.

A: *That beginning is very different from the one I proposed this morning, but the advice to "write every day," "write about what interests you personally," and "write to discover what you think" is certainly part of my message.*

MJ: My way of doing things isn't direct, but it's the primary way that I find the subject that I want to write about. When I locate something that sounds interesting (and increasingly the hunt is stimulated by a conference call for papers, or an invitation to give a talk at another university), I begin to focus in earnest.

At this stage I usually have something five to ten pages in length, a core idea of sorts. Then maybe I'll have another segment of five or six pages that I wrote after reading the original bit; but at this point the two parts don't really connect very well. I read what I have again and again. I rewrite and reread. I chop. Maybe half of what I've written goes, though some bits may turn into other papers. I reread. I write. I chop.

A: *You've said outlines don't help. What about writing to a title, or even an abstract?*

MJ: Your emphasis on starting with a title and abstract isn't helpful to me. I would get in my own way if I worried too much about an abstract, or even a title. I never end up with the framework I thought I was going to use when I began. I guess I have come to accept this and don't even bother about the framework at the beginning, I just wait and see what emerges. It is exciting really, to see what will come of the writing. I always write my abstracts last. Even when a paper begins with a submission to a conference that requires abstracts and titles, what I start with is only marginally connected to what I finally produce. Sometimes I stick with the original title because it appears in a conference program, but I always have to apologize for the misleading title and use a better one when I submit a paper for review.

My titles often change during the revision process as well. I have even had titles rewritten by editors! Titles are important to me only when I get a chance to be provocative with them, but then they usually are not revealing of the content of the paper and so editors don't like my favorite titles. For instance, the article I did in *ASQ* years ago on the physical structure of organizations was titled "When Ears Have Walls," with an appropriately revealing subtitle, of course. *ASQ* hacked off the interesting bit and left the boring part. Likewise, *Organization Studies* eliminated the "Where There Is Smoke" in the title of the paper Sandy Ehrlich and I did on humor as an indicator of paradox and ambiguity. Boring titles don't inspire me and so I see no reason to make them part of my writing process. When I get a good title, the image helps motivate my writing but does not really focus me in any specific way. It more captures the spirit of the piece than anything else. But editors have told me that they find this form of titling distracting, distasteful, demeaning to the seriousness of the endeavor, et cetera.

For me writing is about interacting with ideas. Since most ideas have aspirations of their own, I have to come to terms with them. For me this takes the form of interacting with ideas by writing them out in various ways, introducing them to one another, listening to the ways they interact around me. I realize that I am guilty of gross reification here, but this is how it seems to come about. It's the best description I can give.

A: *So you have several "islands" of promising stuff. Then what?*

MJ: After I have around 15 pages that are marginally useful, I start editing. The rest is pure editing, or at least that is how it feels. I read what I've done. If it's muddy, I try to clarify.

What I'm looking for is something that is exciting and interesting. Every morning I start reading from the beginning and see where I get stuck. That is where I begin my day's writing. Sometimes to fix the next bit requires adjusting what came before and I have to go backward instead of forward. What the paper is about often changes completely in this process.

A: *What are you looking for?*

MJ: It is hard to say, really. I know it when I see it—or hear it is more accurate, I suppose.

A: *It sounds as if you started out with a distinctive style of writing, quite a bit like what many writers of fiction propose, and have been perfecting your approach for some time. Can you identify specific insights along the way that made you more efficient or helped you find the content you were aiming for?*

MJ: Not worrying about efficiency helped. I trust the writing process. That may come from my training in journalism with tight deadlines and constant pressure to pump out text; you learn to trust the writing process implicitly. Otherwise you would lose your mind, I think. But I am no more efficient now than before, really. Maybe I am more effective, if publications per year is the criterion. I can recognize a good argument sooner now, and get ideas interacting with less hesitation. Also, I think having good taste in ideas is important because that way you don't waste time getting lots of rejections for not having anything significant or interesting to say. And at this point in my development, I can keep more projects going at once. This makes my productivity higher.

One aspect of efficiency or something like it may be that I have learned to work through ideas when I am sleeping. This is a big part of my writing and is why getting up early is the hallmark of my writing regimen. Often when I wake up, a solution to the problems I have been struggling with is hanging in the air, and if I wake early and write immediately I can capture it and work it into my paper with all sorts of interesting consequences.

A: *Do you find conversations with others helpful?*

MJ: I do most of my writing in isolation, but the reader is always with me, or I am always the reader, so writing is a conversation of sorts. The ideas I work with are conversing all the time too. So conversation is everywhere a part of my writing.

I suppose you are asking more about conversations with other people, though. I am doing loads of coauthoring these days. I am interested in collaborative work, and collaborating is a big part of the learning I need to do and the reason I am interested in the topic.

Conversation is essential to coauthorship, and the writing process is really just a trace of the conversation. In fact, for me, conversation is the point and the written output just legitimizes the conversation. Writing papers gives license to conversing. This is its joy. But I suppose the writing purpose gives the conversations focus; I guess I am saying that conversation and writing are inseparable, though sometimes I do the whole thing in physical isolation.

Another kind of conversation I use is the kind set up by participating in academic conferences. First, there is the conversation that accompanies all that interaction outside of formal sessions. This may be the best conference conversation. Ideas are thick in the air and everyone has something to say that is interesting. The worst period for me was the time when conferences became a place to meet old friends, and we never seemed to get to interesting discussions. Now, we have become so good at conferencing, we use the time we have for really intense and interesting conversations about our work and where we are headed. If I am stuck writing a particular paper, there will always be somebody I can find to unstick me if I just get to a conference. It is terrific. I go to about five or six conferences a year, and these are very important to my work. In addition to filling me with ideas for writing projects and connecting me with my several coauthors, they structure my writing process. There are deadlines to meet in going to so many conferences that they keep me focused and more productive than I might otherwise be. And having to present my work so often and in so many different ways offers terrific opportunities to experiment with finding good ways to make the case for the ideas I am working with. Presenting is my way of framing arguments. So I guess I do use something like your conversation method, but mine is a live conversation with people I actually meet, versus the conversation that occurs between texts. I have always been fairly literal.

A: *How do you interact with the literature in your field?*

MJ: I am uncertain how I do this. Of course, I skim the major journals in my field regularly, mostly to see who is doing what so when I meet people at conferences I can ask more about something that interests me or would be helpful to my work. It also keeps a buzz in my head about what people are currently talking about. I do loads of reviewing and I am certain this helps with the conversation, as you call it. Giving feedback to others on their work makes me think about the things I am reading in relation to those others are reading, and this produces a kind of interaction with the literature in my field, I suppose. People send me lots of papers too, which I usually have not got the time to read thoroughly, but glancing at them keeps me current. I keep files by topic of new material to read, and when I am writing or preparing a talk or lecture, I try to read a couple of papers to get me started.

Much of my reading is outside of organization theory per se. I read philosophy, literary theory, books on art and artists. At least that is the literature I turn to when I have a moment to ponder and do what I call real reading. This reading supports my research on narrative and other aesthetic approaches to organizations. I also try to read in marketing, communication theory, and strategy a bit, as my research on organizational identity and image increasingly draws me into these fields. But then I have always followed an interdisciplinary path.

When I am writing, I am almost always referring to three or four other texts as the main source of my inspiration. Often my initial writing of those two- or three-pagers was triggered by something I read, and this is how ideas come into the conversation in my head that leads to a paper. Once I have begun a paper in earnest, these will comprise the primary sources on which I draw. By then, references to other people's work come flooding in. As I write particular sentences, I am aware that somebody has said something like this before and I make a reference to their work. Or they have said something I am contradicting and they get a reference for that. As I read and reread my own words, the references just seem to fill themselves in. I must have loads of stuff like this in my head, because I usually have rather long lists of references at the back of my papers. When I am working with coauthors, I get introduced to additional references, and often this leads me to read in new directions. After that, additional interaction with the literature comes from the advice of reviewers who recommend various articles or books to me on the basis of connections they see to my writing and ideas.

A: *I like the "voice" of your work. How do you achieve it? Do you consciously work at it?*

MJ: I read what I write constantly, and listen to the sound of the words. I used to write poetry (badly) and I think it instilled in me a sensitivity and love for words that influence my writing. I edit and edit at the word level, as well as for phrases, sentences, and the rest. Editing at the word level is my favorite. I am very conscious of the words I use.

You can't write poetry without developing an ear for language and its rhythms. There is a rhythm for good academic writing too. This is what is missing from most writing in the field of organization studies, sensitivity to the rhythms of language. Without this I don't see how writers can achieve style. Style gives the impression of a narrator, and constructing a narrator is how you get to voice. But there is more to voice than style. One must find a means of self-disclosure, I believe. Writing should be expressive as well as communicative. When it is, that is when you get an impression of the narrator, of a life behind the words. I think this gives additional insight into the ideas in the work, the interaction between the ideas and the writer, and encourages the engagement of the reader. There is quite a lot of reflexivity for me in this, as I am my constant reader during the writing process.

I also read a great deal of classical and contemporary literature when I was learning to write as an undergraduate, and I used a technique given in one of my creative writing courses to find my style. The technique involved choosing a favorite author, reading all of their work, and copying their style until the notion of style got through. Then you had to find your own voice. William Faulkner was my model and I am still not completely rid of his tendency to use ridiculously long sentences! But I think the technique got me to locate style somehow, and this is part of the answer to your question about how I achieve voice.

A: *Can you say more about how presentation informs your writing?*

MJ: I've found presentations more and more useful. But here again I'm not as structured as I imagine you are. I'll prepare a rather large set of overhead slides and take them along with me. The night before

I present, I go through them and decide which ones I'm really going to use. They're all thoughts on the topic. Just before the talk, I make new progress on organizing those thoughts and this gets put into a nice ordered structure before I give the presentation.

But then when I'm actually giving the presentation, I abandon all structure and just follow my instincts and the flow of ideas. I think this gives a kind of liveliness to the talk. It may be an extension of style. It also helps me to connect with the audience and open myself to their inputs, some of which I seem to sense intuitively, or maybe I gauge them by the looks on faces. Anyway, I think that it promotes engagement with the ideas and with me and stimulates lively discussions, which is the part of presentation work I like best.

I have noticed that the more talks I give, the more a conversational voice develops in my writing, and I like this new development. I find I use the first and second person more and more in my writing, and this matches the subjectivist orientation of much of my research. It works for me, but I think one should be careful about simply applying this as a technique or strategy. Let the voice express the ideas rather than trying to shape the ideas by imposing a voice. I learned this as a developmental process, not as a strategy. There is an important issue of integrity here. Without integrity, what might have been style becomes mere fashion.

A: *That expands my thoughts about writing and conversation, though it sounds pretty scary. Do you prepare more structured materials for your teaching? And how does teaching interact with what you are trying to write?*

MJ: Preparing for teaching these days involves deciding on the general topics to be addressed (this has become pretty standardized, sadly) and then assembling the slides I have prepared over the years that relate to the topics selected. I then try to read one or two recent papers on the topic to bring me up to speed. I go over the slides in my retinue and delete, add, and update as appropriate. Then, before I go into class, I stuff the order of topics I think we should follow in my head, but allow the class to develop along different lines if it wants to do so. That is, I encourage questions and discussion from the class, and if certain ideas lend themselves to an answer I bring out the appropriate slide and we discuss the material at that point. Toward the end of the class, I do a quick review in my head to see what we have not covered and bring us to a conclusion, filling in anything they might need we have not gone over.

These days, I emphasize engagement with ideas and dialogue among class members, and so I try to equalize the relationship between myself and the students. I try to learn in front of them in order to encourage their learning, engage with the ideas actively to help them catch the fever, if you will. You can't do that, I don't think, using standard structured lecturing, so I have tended to move away from this style. Still, I don't do facilitation of discussion much either, I am an active partner. I guess we move toward a leaderless situation more and more, which suits some students better than others. But if you are trying to stimulate and train collaboration and learning, which is how I see my role, perhaps this is a means to that end. I am experimenting, anyway.

A: *Going back to the writing process, what do you do when you're stuck—when what you are working on just doesn't come together?*

MJ: This is not a very big problem for me. As I said before, I have been trained to write to deadlines, and getting stuck just isn't part of the schema. You can always write something, and if you can edit you make it good enough to read and then change some more. The best thing for me to do when nothing much is happening is to put what I am writing aside and do something else for a time. These days I have so many writing projects going on at once that I just go to something else until I can't take that one any further and then I return to the first project.

Another move to make at a sticking point is to pass off to a coauthor. This is a way to get incredible efficiency and creativity into a writing process, if you have a partner with whom you write easily. Majken Schultz and I do this on all our cowriting projects, and I really think some of my best work has been done with her using this interactive style of writing. But you can't do this with just anyone, at least I can't, and you do need periods of intense face-to-face interaction to find your cooperative balance, generate your ideas, and find focus for writing.

A: *Do you find that you are stuck at some points in the writing process more than others?*

MJ: As I said, I don't really get stuck all that much, but I do dislike writing "implications." This has always been difficult for me. How can I know the implications of one of my arguments before it has been published so that I can see what people do with it? This has always puzzled me and makes writing implications seem some-what phony. I have learned to use this section to display all the more speculative portions of my argument, the stuff I want to say that will cause some people to disagree as they read along. If you put this stuff at the end, then reviewers are less likely to throw your whole argument out and reject your paper. It also gives me some-thing to say in the implications section that doesn't leave me feeling like I am making it all up.

A: *Can you say more about the process of working with others? What are the primary benefits of writing with a coauthor? What are the greatest frustrations?*

MJ: More and more I find the joys of writing with others driving out my urge to write alone. I have had a wonderful relationship with Majken Schultz that has, in my view, led to the best theory building efforts I have been involved with to date. I believe that realizing the collaborative potential of learning allowed us to produce work that is certainly above the standard that I have attained working on my own. Besides, it is great fun. Majken and I have similar interests and complementary skills. For instance, she is far more structured than I am, and when we work together we work much more quickly and more along the lines you are talking about. We have an outline! Not that I stick to it, mind you, but there is one.

In a way, our differences give us the best of two worlds. I suppose there are frustrations in this, but they are small in com-parison with the benefits gained. Majken sometimes feels I drag projects out longer than they need to be by suddenly heading off in new directions, taking us away from our original plan. But she usually sees that at least some of these are quite valuable contribu-tions and then she jumps in with extraordinary insights of her own. I really admire her ability to add subtlety and interest to an argument. And she is a great BS detector. If she does not go for an idea, it is usually because it is not worth going for. If I had to figure it out on my own, it would probably take umpteen versions to get rid of it.

My tendency to wordsmith probably gets on Majken's nerves as well, but you will have to ask her about that. I am also too critical. After so many years of writing alone, I sometimes forget that somebody else is writing along with me, and I can be brutal when I think an argument is not well reasoned, I say stuff like "This just doesn't make any sense" or "That section stinks" without thinking about the fact that I am not just talking about my own abilities! But we have learned to accommodate one another's quirks, and what we are able to produce together never ceases to surprise and delight me.

One thing that is really important is that we have developed trust in one another. We have worked together long enough to know that the other person is going to contribute over the long haul, and this allows us the flexibility to get multiple projects done with little hassle. I know if Majken is busy and I jump in and do more than my share on one project, she will more than compensate in another way later on, and vice versa. This has become extremely important now that we are both professors and our multiple commitments are more demanding than ever before. We work together on teaching as well as research, so our collaboration has grown over the years. I can always count on Majken to pull through for me when I just don't think I am going to make it. This is one of the joys of good collaboration and friendship that must emerge from years of working together successfully. You don't do this in a hurry.

But I have found that what I have learned through my work with Majken generalizes, at least somewhat. I have recently had a wonderful experience writing with a new coauthor, Hari Tsoukas. Hari, like Majken, is a pretty structured person and he is also a very good writer. We did a first paper together after several conversations, and I have never experienced a smoother process. We do seem to think along highly similar lines, however, perhaps to an unusual degree. The first time I met Hari, he gave a talk. Afterward I remember thinking with incredulity, I could have given that talk. Then I realized I *did* give that talk only a month or so before I heard his. When we met in my office, we both realized how similar our ideas and approaches were, and we agreed to coauthor a paper. It was a breeze, and we are hopeful of getting it published as we have already gotten encouragement and an invitation to revise. Hari and I are planning additional collaboration in the near future.

I guess what I have learned from these two positive experiences and a couple that were less successful is that I must find someone whose writing practices mesh well with mine. If I am the only person with writing skills on the team, the whole process breaks down for me; the collaborative potential is realized in the writing, and this bit must be shared or it does not work. So one criterion I now set is that I only write with other writers. A second criterion is that a coauthor has to have some significant difference from me. So far, success has come from working with someone who is more structured. When the person I am working with is as unstructured as I am, nothing gets done and great frustration ensues as we lose the potential that drew us to collaborate in the first place. I guess what I am saying is that, although I do not have a structured approach to writing myself and have developed along different lines, I can still benefit greatly from structure, I just have to bring it in from the outside to make it work for me. I am not certain why a structured person would want to take me on as a coauthor. I guess that is a subject for a different interview.

A: *You also paint. In fact, I'm in a rather long line of people who would like to buy something that you've done. How has your interest in visual art affected your writing?*

MJ: Well, what can I say about that? I am keenly aware of composition, line, and color these days as a direct result of my painting. And issues of style and the aesthetic dimensions of experience increasingly occupy my mind. These things are influencing my theorizing about organizations and my approach to doing research and teaching. But if anything, painting and thinking about painting undermine my need to write. They rob me of some of the aesthetic motivation I used to have because I get more pleasure from painting than from writing these days. Partly that is due to overcommitment, which means that writing is becoming more like work and less like exploration as I have to buckle down to meet deadlines. I have to carefully balance my activities. When I first started painting, I stopped writing for several weeks at a time. Now, I have learned to balance these projects, and I think I have found some complementarity. I do not worry so much over the logic of arguments, make connections more easily, and am satisfied with simpler ideas than I used to be. But maybe this is also a function of age and experience. It is hard to tell.

A: *If you were to give this group one or two last pieces of advice, what would they be?*

MJ: For me, writing is both a way of learning and a means to capture learning and pass it on to others. I believe that the most powerful writing is that which emerges from learning processes that are then embedded and celebrated within it. I use an analogy with Chinese painting that was explained to me by Robert Chia. Robert told me that Chinese artists believe that the beauty in a painting is achieved in the visible traces of the brush strokes. The traces of learning left in the best writing are, for me, the beauty and the value of what we do.

A: *Thanks a lot for coming, Jo. I'm rather surprised that this conversation I've billed as "contrarian" has so many points of overlap with my perspective. We agree on writing every day (or as many days as humanly possible), recognizing that what we edit may become part of another paper, "listening" to what we write, and using coauthors as a way of extending our reach. I also suspect that we've let ourselves sound more divergent than we actually are. I do wander in the hope of creative discovery; you use coauthors who are more structured than you are.*

But still your way of writing is very different from mine, and contradicts some of what I've recommended. It's very helpful for you to remind us that there are diverse paths to writing success, and that we each have to discover our own way. In fact, I want to end today's workshop by suggesting to participants that you interview yourselves in the way I've just interviewed Mary Jo Hatch. Ask yourself about your current writing processes, what's best and most frustrating about joint projects, why you get stuck, and what you know about getting unstuck. The complete set of questions I've asked Mary Jo may be helpful. Your current answers will not be your last insights, but it won't surprise you that I strongly believe talking about writing will help you discover, then articulate, what you know, and lead to experimentation that may significantly improve your ability to write well.

Appendix B

⋅⁓§⁓⋅

A Conversation on Writing in English by Non-Native Speakers With Jone Pearce

The globalization of academic conversation is an exciting trend in all scholarly disciplines, but it is not easily accomplished. Scholarship is carried out in different ways in different countries. The larger social, economic, and political setting has an important influence. As I move between the United States and England, I sometimes find these are huge and disconcerting differences, even though they are the reason I made the trip.

My friend Jone Pearce has been doing international research for some time and has worked with writers in Eastern Europe and China. This appendix records our e-mail conversation on some of the special research and writing issues faced by her colleagues trying to publish in English-language journals.

A: *Thanks a lot for taking the time for this conversation, Jone. I am including an appendix on writing for English-language journals by nonnative speakers in this book because I'm enthusiastic about the increasingly pluralistic conversations I encounter. Perhaps we can start with this idea. Can you talk, in generic terms, about what you are learning by going outside of the United States?*

J: Gee, Anne, why not start with an easy question! It is hard to know where to begin. It would have been easier for me to answer this question after my first month living and working outside the United States back in 1989; now my experiences have become so embedded in the way I see the world that it is difficult to isolate what I learned where.

Of the many things I have been learning, one of the most unexpected and personally enjoyable has been learning about how our

143

colleagues and their institutions operate in their very different circumstances. But I would also say that the most important thing to me has been that I have learned about my familiar American world.

A: *I know you've written with colleagues outside the United States. Can you give me a "balance sheet" of the things that have been most rewarding and most difficult about these collaborations?*

J: One of the things I have learned in collaborating with those living with different demands is to contextualize everything. So, I will begin my answer by describing my collaborations. Readers will be able to evaluate my later comments in this light.

I have had many rather casual collaborations with those not trained in the United States, but only a few of these have actually been productive. In my case, this work has been primarily with colleagues in Hungary, Czech Republic, and Lithuania. In retrospect, these collaborations have been successful because we shared the same goal for the collaboration, whether that was producing a case study or developing and publishing new understandings of organizational changes in their countries.

Further, we each brought distinctive capabilities to the relationship—I had experience constructing empirical studies and getting them published in the leading scholarly journals, and my colleagues knew the local people and context we wished to study. We could spend our time arguing about what the project meant and not about who should do what. There is no question that when these relationships were formed back in 1989-1992, I benefited from a situation in which Americans were seen as something new, glamorous, and knowing. Alas, with experience, my colleagues' opinion of Americans has descended to the European norm. Our strengths and weaknesses are all too well known now.

In order to make your balance sheet a little more useful to non-Americans, I want to boldly add to my own account what I believe one of my collaborators might say about the rewards and difficulties of working with an American such as myself. Because I have worked longest and best with Hungarians, I will create a fictitious "Zolt" who will provide his balance sheet for his collaboration with me. (Of course, I have never worked with any Hungarian who would be as impolite as this "Zolt.") Our respective experiences might be summarized in this way:

Jone's Rewards	*Jone's Difficulties*
Learning about people, organizations, and situations which otherwise would be inaccessible.	Investing a lot of time in developing mutual expectations across training, language, and cultural barriers.
Learning to see phenomena from my collaborator's perspective, providing new insights and synergies.	Investing a lot of time in sustaining collaborative relationships across distance and multiple time zones (in my experience, the "building" requires face-to-face time).
Learning to view myself, my organizations, and my situation in a new way.	
Developing an entirely new line of research.	Managing the anger and trying to salvage the collaboration when signals are inevitably missed and expectations are not met.
Presenting research at international conferences, which leads to contacts and learning from additional perspectives in a virtuous circle.	Coping with the frustrations of working within weak and undermining infrastructures in non-rich countries.
Having to spend considerable amounts of time lost and confused—the kind of humbling experience necessary to all tenured professors.	Incurring the expense and personal costs of frequent overseas travel.
Introducing my children to the rewards of living in another country.	
Making new friends and having a lot of fun in societies with different traditions.	

"Zolt's" Rewards	"Zolt's" Difficulties
Learning how to do research and to produce top-tier scholarly papers "in the American style."	Investing a lot of time in developing mutual expectations across training, language, and cultural barriers.
Learning about and making contacts with American people, organizations, and situations which could be very useful to my career.	Investing a lot of time in sustaining collaborative relationships across distance and multiple time zones.
Learning to see phenomena from my collaborator's perspective, providing new insights and synergies.	Managing the anger and trying to salvage the collaboration when signals are inevitably missed and expectations are not met.
Learning to view myself, my organizations, and my situation in a new way.	Sustaining the forbearance to tolerate insensitive foreign collaborators' astonishments and complaints about the way things are done in my country.
Presenting research at American conferences, which leads to additional contacts and learning from new perspectives in a virtuous circle.	Explaining the difficulties of working within weak and undermining infrastructures to a pushy American who expects everything to be done *now*.
Securing a visiting (or eventually a permanent) professorship at an American university (providing better support for a research career and providing cultural opportunities for my children, including learning excellent English).	Taking on Herculean burdens of an ambitious research project in an environment which does not support such work or reward accomplishments.
Making new friends and going out with colleagues who are expecting to have fun.	Working to make sure my own ideas and insights are not left out of the written work due to my lack of language confidence and pushiness.

A: *Your answer makes me realize that the title of this appendix is too narrow. The issues of globalizing academic conversation are as much about our leaving the English-language tradition as they are about making more room for others to enter. Before we talk about writing more specifically, however, I wonder how your experience with "Zolt" and others compares with the work you have done with colleagues in the U.S.*

J: Mulling this over, I think I have had about the same proportion of successful and failed collaborations with American-trained colleagues as with others; but this mental review has revealed to me that I have stronger negative feelings about the failed American collaborations than the non-American ones, and I am puzzling about why that should be. Perhaps the effort involved in establishing cross-national collaborations results in a kind of early elimination of relationships that just aren't going to work before we have become too heavily invested. Or, it could be that our sharp division of labor (and, frankly, ignorance of each other's tasks) provides less ground for disagreement. Or maybe Americans are just more irksome as collaborators. . . .

A: *You've had a chance to look over a draft of this book, and so you know about my emphasis on writing as conversation, the importance of seeking advice, the utility of focusing on a specific set of "conversant" articles, and the helpfulness of looking at exemplar work that delivers a similar message to other audiences. Do you think the same advice is applicable to nonnative writers?*

J: Very much so. Because of the sheer size of the English-reading scholarly audience, colleagues who want their work to be known beyond the small circle of specialists in their country are forced to write, listen, and speak in English. But what I find attractive about your approach is that it helps to clarify that the differences are not just language issues. Language is the easiest hurdle to overcome—translators can be hired everywhere to convert one's ideas into perfect English prose.

The real difficulty is that America and American journals overpower my field, due to size and early dominance. That means that American perspectives and standards domineer many conversations. This is by no means an easy hurdle to overcome. For example, using your framing, one can think of American doctoral programs as intensive five-year immersions in scholarly conversation. Anyone who spends 70 hours a week for five years frequenting the same café, with the same patrons, will become very comfortable with the conversational flow—able to anticipate others' reactions, exchange "in-jokes" with just a few words, and be sensitive to long-standing feuds and affections. Of course, outsiders blundering into this cozy circle will be treated like the tourists they are—either rudely snubbed or patronized (as long as they don't stay too long).

While our non-American-trained colleagues are well aware of their disadvantages in our Americanized field, I think your way of framing writing suggests useful steps they might take to have more success in this café. First, thinking of writing as a conversation can help them focus on being heard. Because what we write is often so central to our sense of self, it is easy to get defensive when we have not been heard, or have been misheard. However, in conversation, we would not think of blabbing on and on when we know we are not being understood; no one wants to be thought a bore. Yet we do find people who write on and on without ever finding a publisher (i.e., someone who thinks what they are saying is worth heeding). Thinking of writing as a conversation helps to direct our attention to fellow conversationalists, to an interchange rather than writing as a display of one's status as an intellectual.

Second, your ideas provide a way of disentangling that which is particular to American culture from that which has arisen because of the large and competitive nature of the scholarly conversation in the United States. The astute reader will have noticed that Hungary, Czech Republic, and Lithuania are all small countries—the scholars in any one field have known one another from their school days. The few universities and institutes are all arrayed in accepted status hierarchies, and the ways they are funded make this hierarchy very stable. By contrast, in the United States there are many, many, universities that have long competed with one another to hire the brightest faculty, who can then attract the best students, and bring in the most government funding.

In this large competitive arena, writing for blind-reviewed publication becomes the most meritocratic means to compete. This means that finding an audience for your writing is very important. There are very powerful incentives to scholars to be successful conversationalists (money, prestige, autonomy, quality of working life), as well as punishments for not succeeding (being fired before tenure, or denigrated as an "old has-been" after tenure). In countries with small scholarly communities, everyone knows who is cleverer than whom, and because there are so few players, the conversations are small and oral. Few who read an individual's written work will not already have heard it discussed, and so the pressure to understand your conversationalists and write for a very competitive market in written work just does not exist. Meanwhile, over the course of an American career, those who face continuous harsh pressures to attract a large number of conversationalists via the written word become better at writing for that demanding and impersonal audience than those who have not faced these pressures. All this creates an impediment to conversation between Americans and non-Americans.

Americans are acutely aware of their performance pressures (and because most only know American work, blind to their own ethnocentrism) and so they tend to see anything from outside their familiar café conversation as rudimentary and self-indulgent. It is often not "on target." Colleagues not trained in American universities are equally alert to the "American-ness" of the leading journals and the sound of in-group jargon, but they often are unable to distinguish the culturally specific from what is necessary to make a work successful in café rough-and-tumble.

For example, I was asked to assist an editor with a manuscript from one of the formerly-Communist European countries. Because I had become more familiar with the conversations in this part of the world I was better able to read past the material not appropriate for a journal publication (for example, a too-detailed revue of introductory literature) and see that the authors had developed an analysis of managerial behavior that was novel and useful. They applied the concept of the "Romantic Hero" myth to their sampled managers' struggle to redefine their roles in a transition economy. While the metaphor of the manager-as-romantic-hero is certainly popular in writings for American managers (just recall all of the sports, military, and cowboy metaphors) a serious analysis of hero metaphors had never been attempted. With a few minor deletions and changes in emphasis, these authors were able to expand and enrich the café conversation.

I don't want to downplay the real problem of ethnocentrism among many American editors. I have read truly vicious assaults on authors for small malapropisms and once had a paper based on Hungarian data rejected because it "wasn't generalizable," whereas that comment has never been made about my American data! Nevertheless, such ethnocentrism can be battled more effectively if it is less confounded by differences due to past conversational experience.

A: *What would you advise people just beginning their careers who wish to (or are now required to) publish in these journals?*

J: Join the conversation! Really immerse yourself in exemplars, as described in Chapter 4. Seek help decoding and interpreting this material. To that end, nearly everyone always has a few American academics passing through each year. Rather than having them just give a talk on their research, ask them to conduct a half-day seminar on publishing in the morning and then present their research in the afternoon. I guarantee you will have a richer conversation about the research after spending the morning together.

On one of my research trips, a Hungarian colleague arranged for me to conduct a five-day residential doctoral seminar on theory testing, measurement, and publishing. I was glad to reciprocate for all the help I'd received, and we all learned a lot. Scholars in any country should remember that visitors make contact because they want to have a richer experience of your country. You should think of ways to pull these visitors into real conversation, not a one-way information flow.

Similarly, before attending a conference, I recommend to all scholars that they look over the list of other attendees and try to read several papers by those whose research is closest to their own. Believe me, there are almost no academics so exalted that they will not be ecstatic that you took an interest in their work and want to discuss common concerns. Small conferences are the best, because you can really get to know the participants over several days. But even large professional meetings can work if you focus on those with common research goals. For example, I had been exchanging papers and e-mail correspondence independently with a colleague from Holland and with one from Israel. Since we had an interest in the same topic, it is not surprising that we all ended up making plans to attend the same meeting. I arranged for us all to have lunch one day, and now the two of them have done a research project together.

It does take time. At large meetings like this, I would advise young scholars to take advantage of preconference consortia or any other activity that will help them to get to know a smaller group of people. They should go to the events organized for newcomers. They should be active on e-mail, but remember that e-mail may be most fruitful if it is supplemented by face-to-face contacts.

A: *Do you have any advice about choosing research and writing partners once an international group of scholars has met in these ways?*

J: Well, writing for the most competitive journals is very difficult and so it probably pays to develop a collaboration with someone who has successfully published in such journals. Be smart! Most American academics haven't published in top journals either, and you could just learn how to publish in third-tier journals if you choose the wrong collaborator. (This is really advice to have high aspirations, whether or not you are working with collaborators.)

Of course, the broader issue is establishing the right intellectual partnership, and I do have some very specific advice. When you do collaborate, never trade away your right to coauthor any papers coming from the collaboration, and try to make sure that enough of your own research interests are included so you will be able to get your own ideas out. Finally, remember that there are many of us. If the first collaboration (or second or third) doesn't work out—try again.

A: *Are there any special issues facing senior scholars who wish to publish in English-language journals?*

J: While all of the above strategies would work for senior scholars, there is a psychological impediment at work. Writing for the most competitive American scholarly journals is a brutal, humiliating business. Some reviewers are unkind, unfair, and just plain wrong! Many senior American scholars who have published enough in those journals to achieve tenure turn their attention to books (where the editors are nicer), to consulting, and to other activities that don't require so much anxiety and degradation.

Since most societies treat their senior scholars with even more respect and deference, after years of such treatment it is very painful to begin the struggle required to publish in the top-tier American scholarly journals. Many such scholars have never had their ideas treated with such brutality, and it can be very insulting indeed.

Then why do it? It is the only sure way to know that your ideas are of real interest to others. It is the only way to communicate with a wide audience.

A: *It sounds to me as if senior scholars from other countries might be well advised to think about book-length manuscripts.*

J: I think that's true. But this is part of the café too, not really a way of opting out of the conversation. Editors give the most attention to people whose work is known by others. Book manuscripts are reviewed. There is still a need to get to know and perhaps work with scholars from English-speaking countries.

The initial contacts among senior scholars are often made at meetings. Visiting scholars can help their colleagues in the countries they visit know which meetings would be most interested in their ideas. And we can make sure we introduce people who attend these meetings for the first time.

It also is necessary to remember that the American scholarly conversation tends to be relatively more impersonal and competitive. One of the ways many scholars have learned to manage this awkward situation is to separate how they interact with people in face-to-face encounters (always courteous) with what they provide in an anonymous written evaluation (a possibly harsh, honest evaluation they feel honor-bound to provide). I advise my students to never assume that because someone has been nice to you he or she will provide a positive confidential evaluation or any other kind of assistance. In other words, it is still difficult.

A: *Do you think that those of us who grew up with English as our first language might learn something new if we sometimes thought about writing as nonnative writers?*

J: Certainly. Learning another language provides great insights into other ways of thinking and perceiving the world, as well as a lens into another society. However, you cannot focus on learning a new language orally; it is also necessary to read and write in it to get scholarly dividends.

There are benefits to be gained even by those who do not take on this difficult task. An example of the rich insights that can be gained from focusing on language comes from my work with colleagues translating questionnaires. We always develop them first in English, our common language, and I have always worked with colleagues on translations, never professional translators. Here's a story that shows why. I am interested in the extent and role of informal personal relationships in organizations that don't have a strong modernist tradition of bureaucratic impersonalism. One of the questions on interviews and questionnaires asks about the role that nepotism plays in raises, task assessments, hiring, and promotion. The word *nepotism* translates straightforwardly into Hungarian as *családi össze-fonódások*, with the same direct meaning and subtle emotional connotations. However, the word does not exist in Lithuanian. The concept had to be explained in a long awkward phrase. Certainly, if a people do not have a common word for something, they probably see less of it, or at least are less attuned to it, than those for whom it is a familiar concern. Since I had trouble believing that nepotism could be so alien, my Lithuanian colleague and I spent hours exploring this difference in our respective workplaces; we both learned a great deal from one untranslatable word.

But again, I would reiterate that an attraction of your conversational framework is that it directs our attention away from a focus on language toward interaction with others. People can converse, can understand one another with surprisingly little common language. In a conversation, body language and affect can signal a great deal. And you can keep trying, keep rephrasing and reapproaching an issue until you do understand one another. When colleagues converse with limited common language, they may miss each other's clever wordplay and literary references, but if they stick with each other long enough, they can learn things of much greater value than they can from the same old café conversation.

A: *I love your image of an intellectual café. It's a nice equalizer too. Americans are getting enthused about café life, and coffeehouses are booming, but still we are neophytes in this arena. We tend to duck in and out too fast for our "coffee to go."*

We're typically more relaxed when we go to cafés in other countries, even on business. We slow down a bit, are more reflective. I

*hope that the globalization of scholarship will have the same bene-
ficial effect on my intellectual life. I value the philosophical bent of
many non-U.S. colleagues, for differences in values and emotional
response as well as observation. I hope your comments make these
and other contributions to scholarly conversation more likely and
want to thank you again for your insights, Jone. I look forward to
the next time we talk, over a cup of coffee.*

J: I am looking forward to that cup of coffee—but we will have to do
it the Hungarian way in which we both fight-to-the-death for the
check. My severely underpaid colleague would tell the story of
dining with Americans who didn't understand this ritual, and so
gave up too soon and let the impoverished Hungarian pay. Needless
to say, he had to learn cultural adaptation quickly if he didn't want
his children to starve!

Appendix C

❖❖❖

Reviewing Checklist

KURT HEPPARD

This "Reviewing Checklist" is provided to help you assess the overall quality of a scholarly paper or manuscript. I've constructed it from writing and research classes taken with Anne Huff and Chris Koberg at the University of Colorado, then supplemented it by looking at instructions to reviewers from several journals in my field.

Although this is a relatively mechanistic and simplistic system, it has been effective in helping authors make sure that they have not missed important items that reviewers are likely to look for. It can be used early in the writing process (as an outline is being developed) or much later in critiquing finished drafts and resubmissions.

Because this is a generic checklist, some categories may not be relevant to the paper you are considering and you may have other categories or comments to add. In addition, a low rating may or may not indicate a weak paper. Conversely, a high rating may not indicate a strong paper. You will still have the difficult task of drawing together an overall assessment and considering the paper's contribution.

I use the list to systematically remind myself (as author or reviewer) of potentially important categories of scholarly writing. Then I step back to take a more holistic view of the paper. Rather than overwhelm myself and others with detail, I emphasize the most important strengths and weaknesses of the paper I'm considering, and suggest specific steps for improvement as I complete my review. I also try to do this in a way that supports ongoing community, following the guidelines found in Chapter 1 of this book.

The checklist is divided into seven parts:

1. Introductory Elements
   - Summarizing the paper
   - Title
   - Abstract
   - Introduction
   - Connection with previous conversation
2. Questions for Quantitative Papers
   - Theoretical framework and development of hypotheses
   - Description and evaluation of methods
   - Results
3. Questions for Qualitative Papers
4. Questions for Theory Development
5. Questions for Case Studies
6. Discussion
7. Conclusion

Use the following categories to rate each question. All nonapplicable questions should be left blank.

1. Not at all.
2. Only to a limited extent.
3. At an acceptable level.
4. To a significant extent.
5. Completely.

Introductory Elements	*1*	*2*	*3*	*4*	*5*
Summarizing the paper:					
Can you identify the one or two main points of the paper?					
Is the target journal an appropriate outlet for the paper?					
Title:					
Does the title grab attention and say something important about the paper?					
Does it include important words that will index the paper appropriately?					
Abstract:					
Is the abstract compelling? Does it attract attention?					
Does it provide an accurate overview of the paper?					
Does the abstract summarize major accomplishments?					
Does it identify the central theory or literature stream or "conversation"?					
Does the abstract inform the reader about critical features of the article (methodology, data sources, and so on)?					
Does it use relatively simple words and sentences?					
Can the abstract be understood without reading the paper?					
Does the order of the abstract reflect the order of the paper?					
Introduction:					
Does the introduction entice the reader to read on?					
Does it establish a need for the paper by highlighting gaps or disagreements in the literature?					
Does it organize ideas and material in a logical and meaningful sequence, which is then reflected in the body of the paper?					
Does it introduce key concepts from the paper?					
Does it highlight the key contribution or "value added" by the paper?					
Connection with previous conversation:					
Are antecedents of the paper clearly identified?					
Is the discussion of previous work an appropriate length?					
Is the author's intended contribution to previous conversation clearly identified? Are key terms defined?					
Would a significant number of scholars in the field find the paper's subject and approach interesting?					

1 = Not at all   2 = Only to a limited extent   3 = At an acceptable level   4 = To a significant extent
5 = Completely

Questions for Quantitative Papers	1	2	3	4	5
Theoretical framework and development of hypotheses (if appropriate):					
Are the study's propositions and hypotheses clearly articulated?					
Are the basic arguments of the paper important and interesting?					
Are important premises and assumptions identified?					
Is there a graphic depiction of the relationship between key variables in the paper?					
Are key terms defined?					
Would a significant number of scholars in the field find the paper's subject and approach interesting?					
Description and evaluation of methods (if appropriate):					
Is the methodology of the paper clearly identified?					
Are data collection methods described adequately?					
Are the sampling strategy and sample explained?					
Is the operationalization of variables and constructs plausible (content validity)?					
Are dependent variables identified and described?					
Are independent variables identified and described?					
Are control variables identified and described?					
Do measures theoretically relate independent and dependent variables (construct validity)?					
Are control variables used effectively?					
Are questionnaire or other measurement items identified and described?					
Was the discussion of interview or questionnaire construction and response rates clear and comprehensive?					
Have steps been taken to avoid data collection errors?					
Is there evidence of reliability or internal consistency in the study?					
Results:					
Are the findings adequately and accurately described?					
Are results clearly related back to original propositions, hypotheses, research questions, and data analysis?					
Do tables provide sufficient and accurate data to allow the reader to reach independent conclusions?					
Are figures and appendixes used effectively?					
Is implied causality justified?					
Has the author adequately considered alternative explanations for the results found?					

1 = Not at all   2 = Only to a limited extent   3 = At an acceptable level   4 = To a significant extent
5 = Completely

Questions for Qualitative Papers	1	2	3	4	5
Is the purpose of the research adequately established?					
Are the duration and intensity of observation clear?					
Are the nature of the site, and key players, adequately discussed?					
Are methods of collecting and analyzing data adequately described?					
Does the writer convince the reader that he or she was able to gather information about key events from appropriate sources?					
Is there evidence that informants trusted the researcher and were likely to honestly share information with the researcher?					
Has the author adequately considered alternative interpretations of the data presented?					
Is there evidence of systematically considering evidence that contradicts the author's interpretations?					
Has the author adequately considered alternative interpretations of the data presented?					
Is there evidence of systematically considering evidence that contradicts the author's interpretations?					
Questions for Theory Development	1	2	3	4	5
Is the purpose of the research adequately established?					
Is the need for (or purpose of) theory development well established?					
Is previous theory adequately summarized?					
Is the author's contribution to theory significant?					
Is it well organized and clear?					
Is it adequately linked back to the literature?					
Questions for Case Studies	1	2	3	4	5
Is the "story" intrinsically interesting?					
Is sufficient background information provided?					
Are key issues clearly stated?					
Is there enough information to develop alternative scenarios about future development?					
Is there enough information to allow reader to recommend an action and discuss possible consequences of that action?					

1 = Not at all   2 = Only to a limited extent   3 = At an acceptable level   4 = To a significant extent
5 = Completely

Introductory Elements	1	2	3	4	5
Is there enough information to develop relatively detailed implementation plans for the recommended action or decision?					
Is there enough information to allow the recommended action and its implementation plan to be discussed and analyzed?					
Discussion	1	2	3	4	5
Does the discussion section introduce new and relevant topics? (It should not simply restate findings.)					
Does the discussion section use consistent terminology that is understandable in the context of the entire paper?					
Are limitations of the study clearly stated?					
Are logical extensions of this study and avenues of additional research provided?					
Conclusion	1	2	3	4	5
Does the conclusion retain the reader's interest in the subject and the paper itself?					
Are the most important components and contributions of the study highlighted?					
Is there something new in the conclusion that has not appeared elsewhere in this paper?					
Would the busy reader looking only at the introduction and conclusion understand the contribution of the paper?					

1 = Not at all   2 = Only to a limited extent   3 = At an acceptable level   4 = To a significant extent
5 = Completely

Appendix D

✦✦✦

*Exercise Summary/
Semester Course Outline*

As mentioned in the Preface, the exercises in this book have been used in various teaching formats, from one-day workshops to a semester-long track in a PhD seminar that also considers a substantive topic. This appendix summarizes all of the writing exercises in this book by chapter heading, and indicates which week of a semester course would be devoted to each chapter.

In a short course, I have students arrive the first day with three topics they are currently writing about or are interested in writing about. This assignment is given even if the course includes people who have just started graduate work and have little scholarly experience to draw upon in identifying writing projects. The session typically focuses on the following:

- Brief individual presentation of these alternatives to the entire class (which is also a good way for participants to get to know each other)
- Presentation of the "critical diamond" found in Chapter 3
- Individual analysis of each of their topics in the four areas of evaluation, then discussion in small groups
- My comments on common dilemmas based on eavesdropping on the group
- Work on title and abstract for the one topic that the participant chooses

In a longer course, I introduce the substantive subject I am writing in the first few weeks of the course while students think a bit about three subjects for the third week of class. Typically, I discuss brainstorming techniques in the first session and encourage people to come see me if they are having problems, so everyone arrives at the third session with a set of alternatives they are reasonably happy with. I focus on helping students find realistic projects that are likely to result in a complete draft before the semester is over.

In the ensuing weeks, I assign most but not all of the exercises listed below. Exercises that take a week or more should be completed by the week the chapter is to be discussed. Most of these are covered by conversation with the whole class. The instruction to "seek the advice of others" is typically accomplished within small group sessions during the class period. I no longer try to group students by their subject of interest; instead, I use a variety of devices to vary group membership over time. Thus, by the end of the course, when presentations are made, members of the class have some familiarity with all projects in the course.

Week 1: In a semester-long class, I emphasize the subject matter of the course in the first few weeks and give less attention to writing. The first day typically ends by talking about the writing segment of the course and having a large group discussion of Exercises 2 and 3 after students have taken a few minutes to think of answers to these questions on their own. Exercises 1 and 4 are their homework for the next time we meet.

Chapter 1. Writing as Conversation

EXERCISE 1
(Homework for Week 2)

*Identify the people, topics, and specific
works that provide the intellectual
foundation of your project.*

EXERCISE 2
(5-10 minutes in class)

*Identify potential members of your
"writing community."*

EXERCISE 3
(5-10 minutes in class)

*Think of at least three things you can do to form
and then sustain your writing community.*

Week 2: The beginning of the semester is always crowded with house-keeping tasks and I used to wait to get the writing assignment off the ground until other aspects of the course were established. I've now decided that graduate students need to prepare for the rewriting that publication requires. The first assignments in my courses are thus devoted to a fast start that will allow students to complete two drafts in one semester. The exercises I assign could focus on the specific subject matter of the course and thus provide useful information for class interaction. An alternative I usually choose is to let people define their own areas of interest in the hope that they will have maximum energy for the hard writing tasks ahead.

Chapter 2. Managing Scholarship

EXERCISE 4
(1 week)

*Summarize the history and anticipated future of one of
your most recent writing projects by charting its
"accordion path."*

EXERCISE 5
(5-10 minutes in class)

*Identify the times, places, and conditions that most
facilitate your writing.*

EXERCISE 6
(10 minutes in class)

*Identify strategies for protecting and enhancing your
writing times.*

Week 3: At the end of this session, I hope that students either commit to a topic or do further brainstorming in a more specific area and make a decision before the next class. Some office hour discussions may be needed over the next few weeks, but I have found that almost all students can find acceptable subjects within the first few weeks of a semester class. If necessary, I note that the purpose of the course is to learn about writing, and thus the perfect topic does not have to be identified. But I try to get students to find a topic that genuinely interests them—a theme found throughout the material that follows.

Chapter 3. Choosing a Topic

EXERCISE 7
(1 week)

Identify basic categories and alternatives within categories that could be used to define your scholarly work.

EXERCISE 8
(First 2 weeks of class)

Generate five to ten ideas for writing projects.
Reduce them to your three top choices, synthesizing your best ideas from the larger set.

EXERCISE 9
(20 minutes in small groups)

Evaluate your top three possibilities for writing on the four points of the critical diamond.
After discussing your alternatives with others, commit to one project as the focus of your immediate attention.

Week 4: It is often hard for students to find their true conversants; they may begin by identifying work that is too general or work outside their field. I talk about conversants from the beginning of the course so that students waste less time when they get to these three assignments but they may take more than one week to complete.

Chapter 4. Identifying Conversants

EXERCISE 10
(1 week)

Identify the three or four written works you would like to be the primary conversants for your paper.

EXERCISE 11
(1 week)

Identify the three or four findings from your scholarly work that would interest the conversants you have identified.

EXERCISE 12
(1 week)

Identify a primary and a secondary target journal.
Copy the first page of several articles from each journal that interests you.
Discuss the logic of your choices, using the first pages as evidence, with others.

Week 5: Exercises 13-15 are often more revealing than students anticipate. As they try to find exemplars, many realize that they have not yet defined the kind of paper they want to write. Once they do, they are often surprised by how many examples they can find.

There is rarely enough time to discuss these works in class. Typically, we talk in a general way about what was learned, or I break the class into smaller discussion groups.

Chapter 5. Using Exemplars

EXERCISE 13
(1 week)

*Describe what you hope to accomplish in your writing
project in at least three different ways.
Settle on one succinct description.
Seek advice about this objective from advisers
and your writing community.*

EXERCISE 14
(1 week)

*Identify four or five exemplars of the kind
of paper you want to write.
If necessary, seek advice about the fit between these
exemplars and your project, then settle on a final group of
two or three works.*

EXERCISE 15
(1 week)

*Outline in detail each exemplar in your
final set, noting the proportion of the text devoted
to each topic.
Also make notes about the "tone" used
in your exemplar.
Draw conclusions about the tacit rules for this kind of
contribution to scholarly conversation.*

EXERCISE 16
(15 minutes in small groups)

*Identify the aspects of each exemplar that are particularly
effective, and any that are ineffective, for communicating
the author's purpose.*

Week 6: Over time, I have become more and more impressed with the utility of the exercises found in Chapter 6. Title and abstract are short but critical parts of a paper that make it relatively easy to focus on the key questions of writing: Who are you trying to talk to? What do you have to say?

Students are asked to come to class with four copies of their title and abstract for distribution, plus a copy on acetate for overhead projection. I divide them into groups and have students in group A exchange copies of their work with group B. (In general, there are three people in each group. I create as many groups as necessary.) Each member of a group reads the titles and abstracts the group received from all members of the other group. Then the group discusses their individual comments until they agree on the most important advice the author should be given. The groups then get together to share this advice.

While this is happening, I make comments on the acetate version. When the class reconvenes, we consider common problems they have observed. Typically, first abstracts are too vague. They include unnecessary words. Often they use jargon. Many do not tell the reader what is most interesting about the paper. It helps to have tangible examples and to try to make them better. Often I encourage students to "get mad" when I say that I don't think I'm going to read on. When I push, they usually come up with something much more interesting.

Chapter 6. Title and Abstract

EXERCISE 17

(1 week or 10 minutes in small groups)

Come up with at least three titles for your work.
Under each, write at least two things
in favor of using the title and two things that
make it less suitable as the most salient
representative of your work.
Discuss this list with others.
Then decide on the working title of your paper.

EXERCISE 18
(1 week)

Even if your intended outlet does not require it, identify three to five key words that convey the most important topics of your paper.

EXERCISE 19
(1 week)

Write an abstract of no more than 150 words for your paper.

EXERCISE 20
(30 minutes in class)

Give several strangers your title, abstract, and key words.
Ask what they think your paper is about.
What would interest them most about such a paper?

Week 7: Sometimes I exchange outlines in the same way that I exchange titles and abstracts. Other times I create dyads of students with similar interests and have them give each other advice outside of class; then we discuss the advice they are giving and getting in a generic way during class time.

Chapter 7. Making an Outline (Really!)

EXERCISE 21
(1 week)

Establish the major and secondary headings of your paper using tertiary headings as needed.
Seek advice on the logic, sequence, and emphasis of your outline from others.
Expand the introduction and conclusion by writing topic sentences for each paragraph.

Week 8: As the volume of students' written work increases, I often
have them distribute copies of their work a day or two before
class so that the advice given in group exercises can be more
detailed and thought out. I may make an acetate overhead of
some of this material so I can lead discussion about common
problems by referring to specific examples.

Chapter 8. Introduction and Conclusion

EXERCISE 22
(1-2 weeks)

Draft the introduction to your paper.
Critique it yourself, then ask others for their advice.

EXERCISE 23
(1 week)

Before you finish your analysis and writing, draft the
conclusion of your paper, going beyond what you are sure
of to experiment with the most assertive statement of the
paper's benefits that you can make.

Week 10 or 13: If I decide to have students prepare a presentation
before their first full draft, I do it about Week 10. As things get
tight in a semester, it is tempting to forgo presentation altogether, but I hate to do that because presentation is usually an
intense learning experience. Therefore, if students move from
outline to a full draft, I make the rough draft due in Week 11
and try to squeeze a presentation assignment into Week 13.

Chapter 9. Presentation

EXERCISE 24
(2 weeks)

Prepare a 10-minute presentation in the format
appropriate for a group you might actually address. If at
all feasible in this scenario, prepare up to ten overhead
slides, with at least two backups for discussion.

Formally present this work to others and ask
for their critique.

Week 11 or 13: Although I make writing part of courses that also cover a specific topic, often the class does not meet for a week or two before their first full draft so that students are free from reading assignments and lectures. If they present in Week 10, I wait until about Week 13 to ask for these drafts. If they move from the title, abstract, and outline to the paper easily, I move the work period up and ask for drafts at about Week 11 so they will have time to exchange papers, digest advice, and prepare a presentation before a second draft is due.

Chapter 10. Body of the Paper/First Full Draft

EXERCISE 25
(1 week)

Carefully read each of your conversant works.
Write as many comments in the margins as possible,
striving to match every detail of their work with details
from your own thinking and research.

EXERCISE 26
(3 weeks)

Prepare a complete draft of your paper over the next three
weeks, then take a week to edit your efforts.

EXERCISE 27
(10 minutes in class)

Reanalyze your writing habits and your writing strengths
and weaknesses so that you can speed and improve
subsequent writing.

EXERCISE 28
(1-2 weeks)

Find several peers with whom to exchange first drafts.

Provide each other with written comments focused on overall structure and message.
As the recipient of advice, decide how you will revise your paper, discussing your revision plan with someone who was not part of the review process, if possible.

Week 16: It is hard for students to complete their second drafts by the end of the semester, and typically we do not discuss their efforts in class. I make a second set of comments and offer each student suggestions for what he or she might do before submitting the paper. Ideally, students also receive comments from several classmates.

Although I push all semester for submission, we make a joint decision at the end of the course about whether it is time to send the paper on for formal review. It doesn't make sense to "burn" this opportunity on a product that is not ready, and it is not fair to our reviewing colleagues to clog the pipeline with manuscripts that obviously need more work.

Chapter 11. Revision, Submission, Revision, and Publication

EXERCISE 29
(2 weeks)

Prepare a second draft to exchange for review, making sure that it is a complete draft with all tables, figures, and bibliography.
Prepare a formal written review of the papers you receive for review.
Make a formal response to the reviews you receive as author, then redraft your paper.

EXERCISE 30

Submit your paper, exactly following submission guidelines, with a brief cover letter.

Appendix E

❖

Advice Summary

To add a little drama, I talk about "blinding flashes of insight" when I teach about writing. They are pretty obvious throughout this text but perhaps the most salient areas are worth repeating here.

1. Writing is conversation—you are unlikely to be published if you are talking to yourself.
2. Writing is a form of thinking that is intrinsic to scholarship; ideally, it is not something put off until the end of a scholarly project.
3. Writing will go more quickly and smoothly if you actively use your management skills (when, where, what materials, and so on)— otherwise it is likely to be driven out by all the things that you and others are managing.
4. Advice from others is critical to successful scholarship: It is easier to get if the demands are modest; it is easier to use if sought early.
5. Straightforward styles typically suit academic conversation best, although there are some notable exceptions.
6. It is necessary to actively choose to write; people who publish have put aside other scholarly and leisure activities.

As the book progresses, a more specific account of writing as scholarship is summarized in the abstracts that introduce each chapter and in the chapter headings themselves. By and large, this is an account of writing and the writing process that can be found in a variety of outlets. The advice bulletins along the way highlight more idiosyncratic opinions that I have seen less often but that have helped me. More detail can be found in the chapter noted.

Here is an overview.

Chapter 1. Writing as Conversation

Think before you write.
Then, write to help you rethink.

You should anticipate making an impact in the
scholarly conversation of your field, from the very
beginning of your career.

Ask for advice often, but keep requests to read an entire
manuscript to a minimum.

Chapter 2. Managing Scholarship

Although writing is time-consuming and difficult, you
should anticipate getting better at it and discovering
more pleasure in it.

Chapter 3. Choosing a Topic

Establish a "bottom drawer" to file project possibilities.
Wait until you have a half-dozen or so before you
synthesize and evaluate them.

Do what really interests you—within reason.

Put all relevant ideas into your current project; do not
ration good ideas in the hope of second publication.

Be interesting, but don't try to be avant-garde
on every dimension.

Chapter 4. Identifying Conversants

Identify conversants who will help you focus on your
main field of scholarship!

Getting mad can help you make choices.

Chapter 5. Using Exemplars

Never lie. Say exactly what you did, and why.

Chapter 6. Title and Abstract

Imagine your readers. Put yourself in their place.

This is your expanded set of conversants:
Short sentences.
Present tense.
Active voice.
Simple constructions.
No more than two instances of the same word.

Chapter 7. Making an Outline (Really!)

Be innovative with form and content, but only
with a purpose.

Cut the first part of your outline.
Think about beginning with your current conclusion.

Chapter 8. Introduction and Conclusion

Speak to a supportive, but somewhat skeptical
(or distracted) friend.

If you can't naturally cite your conversants and several
papers from your target journal in the first few paragraphs
of your paper, rethink your target and/or your conversants.

Curb "pack rat" tendencies.

Avoid the temptation to coin new terms.

Chapter 9. Presentation

Try presenting before your first written draft.

Stop analyzing and writing in time to develop
a good presentation.

Chapter 10. Body of the Paper/First Full Draft

Keep a "dump" at the end of your computer file for material that must be pruned.

Always leave something easy to write as a warm-up task for the next day.

When a writing project is hot, keep working!

Chapter 11. Revision, Submission, Revision, and Publication

Don't fall in love with anything you have written. Be willing to cut, revise, and reorganize every word of every draft.

Never submit an unfinished work "just to see the comments."

Celebrate submission as a victory in itself. Take time off; tidy your desk.

Never resubmit without redrafting.

❧❧

Annotated Bibliography

Kurt Heppard[1]

Becker, H. S., & Richards, P. (1986). *Writing for social scientists.* Chicago: University of Chicago Press.

This book has its origins in a seminar about writing for graduate students in the social sciences. In the process of creating and presenting the seminar, Howard Becker gained a unique under-standing of academic writing as a social activity. This book is valuable for new and established writers in the social sciences because it balances a skeptical and sometimes humorous view of academic writing with useful suggestions about how to avoid common stumbling blocks such as writer's block, revision aver-sion, and a generic writing style. Becker and coauthor Pamela Richards offer examples rather than rules and personal suggestions rather than regulations throughout the text. The authors stress the process and practice of effective academic writing and emphasize the importance of developing good writing habits that will lead to good scholarship.

Brannigan, A. (1981). *The social basis of scientific discoveries.* Cambridge: Cambridge University Press.

This book helps readers decide what might be considered a scien-tific discovery or contribution, how these take place, and how contributions are recognized. It focuses on the very basis of scien-tific discovery and is likely to be useful to scholars and students. Brannigan describes mentalistic and cultural classifications of theo-ries and points out empirical and methodological problems that require a new way of thinking about scholarship. He offers a

177

sociological approach that focuses on the processes that identify and recognize certain scientific accomplishments as "discoveries."

DeBono, E. (1995). *Serious creativity.* London: HarperCollins.

DeBono is a well-known advocate of creative thinking who consults widely and has written many books. This one goes far beyond the "brainstorming" techniques he helped popularize in the 1960s. I especially like the summary of "Six Hats" that the creative person wears at different times to attend to data, include feelings and hunches, be critical, be optimistic, look for additional opportunities, summarize, and think about use (Anne Huff).

Dillard, A. (1989). *The writing life.* New York: Harper & Row.

Writing is often a lonely task and writers will enjoy this book because it provides a collection of thoughts, metaphors, and anecdotes about life as a writer. Annie Dillard offers some technical advice but focuses primarily on providing a great deal of moral support for authors struggling to get through a book, chapter, or even a paragraph. By sharing her writing experiences, as well as the experiences of many famous authors, Dillard shows how the writing life is an exciting journey with many travelers rather than a solitary and isolated existence.

Golden-Biddle, K., & Locke, K. D. (1997). *Composing qualitative research.* Thousand Oaks, CA: Sage.

Describing the results of qualitative research can be particularly difficult. Writers must convert huge quantities of data into coherent manuscripts. This book uses the metaphor of the story to provide insights to those who write about qualitative research. It discusses the important elements of this research story in great detail and includes examples from major management journals including the *Academy of Management Journal and Administration Science Quarterly.* The book describes how authors can get their qualitative research stories published and how authors can successfully revise their stories to meet the concerns of editors.

Hammond, P. E. (Ed.). (1964). *Sociologists at work.* New York: Basic Books.

In this set of essays or "chronicles" by noted sociologists, Phillip Hammond exposes us to the personal side of writers as they describe, in their own words, the process underlying their development of well-known ideas in sociology. Although most students and scholars in the social sciences have read some or all of the works described in this book, few know the inside, introspective view of the scholars who have written these classics. Sometimes we lose sight of the scholar and remember only the impressive work he or she has created. Hammond provides a fascinating volume that drives home the important role that individual perception and preconceptions hold for writers in the social sciences. He makes it easier for both established and novice writers to grasp the critical role that their approach to research and view of the world play in the very social activity of social research.

Hull, D. E. (1988). *Science as a process.* Chicago: University of Chicago.

In developing an approach to scholarly writing, it is important to understand how scientific theories and concepts become accepted by the scholarly community. In this book, David Hull describes an evolutionary process in the development of new ideas that is both competitive and cooperative. Scholars are rewarded not only for being first with new verifiable concepts (competition) but also by describing their work and behaving in such a way that other theorists and researchers will accept these new ideas and integrate them with other emerging scholarship (cooperation). Hull's view is that personal biases, commitments, and self-interest are not only the norm in research but that these characteristics enhance the growth of scholarly conversation and scientific knowledge.

Koberg, D., & Bagnall, J. (1976). *The universal traveler.* New York: William Kaufman.

I taught a course that used this book as one of its texts some time ago. It's a lighthearted but broad guide to thinking creatively and effectively in many different contexts. You may not be able to find it. It's in this bibliography as a reminder that creativity can be applied to all aspects of life, and that "how-to" books that take this approach can enrich writing indirectly as well as directly (Anne Huff).

Kuhn, T. S. (1970). *The structure of scientific revolutions.* Chicago: University of Chicago Press.

This is a landmark book with broad appeal. Kuhn attacks the widely accepted logical empiricist view of science and develops an alternative paradigm in which nonrational approaches have greater influence. He argues that scientific discovery does not take place in a linear, well-ordered manner. Instead, Kuhn points to the critical importance of intellectually violent revolutions that change the prevailing worldview.

Lamott, A. (1994). *Bird by bird*. New York: Pantheon.

> It's not often that a successful writer takes the time to tell you "every single thing" she or he knows about writing but in this very personal account of her writing and life, Anne Lamott does. The book is much like her writing classes and takes the reader all the way from "shitty first drafts" to successful publication and exposes the truths and the myths in between. The book is funny, frank, touching, and throughout gives potential writers insights into the actual process of telling the stories they have always wanted to tell. It helps remind us that good writing is about telling the truth and it is best to approach the writing life with both reverence and a good sense of humor.

McGrath, J. E., Martin, J., & Kilka, R. A. (1982). *Judgment calls in research*. Beverly Hills, CA: Sage.

> This volume is part of the Sage series "Studying Organizations," which discusses innovations in the field of organizational research. In this monograph, the authors provide ideas that challenge the rational model of organizational research offered in many traditional research methodology texts. It helps us to understand what scholars actually do rather than what they are supposed to do. Among other interesting chapters, it describes dilemmas that researchers face as they try to maximize some academic virtues but have to sacrifice others. This book is important because it can help liberate emerging scholars from the bonds of traditional, sometimes stifling, notions of sound research.

Moxley, J. M. (1992). *Writing and publishing for academic authors*. Lanham, MD: University Press of America.

> This is one of the few books available that makes scholarly publishing understandable and accessible. As editor, Moxley has collected the ideas of distinguished scholars and editors who comment on the process of academic writing. The book offers suggestions on how to develop successful writing habits and on how to elaborate, cultivate, and publish scholarly ideas. It provides insights into what the editors of scholarly journals are looking for in manuscripts and how you might attract their attention. It describes how conference proceedings can be organized into a book and how to select the appropriate publishing outlet for your scholarly work. For authors just beginning a scholarly investigation, the book introduces the important questions to consider when developing a research design and methodology. It also discusses strategies for successful collaboration in scholarly writing.

Rudestam, K. E., & Newton, R. R. (1992). *Surviving your dissertation: A comprehensive guide to content and process.* Newbury Park, CA: Sage.

Perhaps the most daunting research and writing project faced by most academic writers is their dissertation. This book discusses both the process and the content of dissertation writing and provides a strategy for success. The authors use examples from several disciplines to illuminate the dissertation process. The book reviews common research issues such as how to select a topic for your dissertation, review the existing literature, develop an appropriate research methodology, and present findings. It makes a unique contribution by discussing strategies for selecting and managing a research committee, dealing with mental blocks and burnout, and managing the anxiety and self-doubt that are common in dissertation research.

Sabin, W. A. (1992). *The Gregg reference manual* (7th ed.). New York: Glencoe/McGraw-Hill.

The intended audience for this 500-page paperbound book is "anyone who writes, edits, or prepares final copy for distribution or publication," which is no overstatement. The book covers both business and academic worlds—including the changes brought about by the pervasive influence of computers and evolving language use and forms. Rules and exceptions are described in a very practical way. A page devoted to the nuances of the semicolon, for example, notes that "mastery over the rules . . . depends . . . on cultivating a sensitivity to the way a sentence moves and the way it sounds." If you have just one reference book on grammar and punctuation, this should be it (Connie Luoto).

Smedley, C. S., Allen, M., & Associates. (1993). *Getting your book published.* Newbury Park, CA: Sage.

Being able to write well and being able to get that writing published are arguably two separate skills. This volume, which is part of the Sage series "Survival Skills for Scholars," focuses on very practical advice for writers trying to get their scholarly work published. The book systematically describes the motivation to write and publish, selecting a publisher, developing a prospectus, surviving the review process, negotiating a good contract, and working with an editor. The book then advises those fortunate enough to have their work under contract to understand the production process so they can be helpful along the way and work with the publisher in marketing the book. The most common pitfalls and problems in publishing are described so that relatively inexperienced authors can avoid learning these difficult lessons through costly experience.

Stinchcombe, A. L. (1968). *Constructing social theories.* New York: Harcourt, Brace & World.

> Almost all of us have been told that good scholarship begins with good theory. However, the origin of good theory often remains a mystery to those entering a scholarly career. How do we invent theories that will support our explanations of social phenomena? In this book, Arthur Stinchcombe describes logical strategies to construct the theories that are the foundation of scholarly writing. The book begins with simple theoretical arrangements and, chapter by chapter, describes more complex theoretical structures. By the end of the book, conscientious readers are likely to be rewarded with greater insight into theory building and should find the daunting challenge of developing logical forms of explanation and constructing concepts more within their reach.

Suppe, F. (Ed.). (1977). *The structure of scientific theories.* Urbana: University of Illinois Press.

> "What is the structure of a scientific theory?" This is a challenging question that serves as the focus for this expansive volume that presents the views of noted scholars who act as proponents or critics of traditional and alternative views of scientific analysis. For readers who are serious about developing an understanding of philosophical thinking about the structure of scientific theory, this book is a valuable and thought-provoking resource.

Tufte, E. R. (1983). *The visual display of quantitative information.* Cheshire, CT: Graphics Press.

> Perhaps the greatest challenges in presenting charts or graphs are, to be totally honest, to hold the interest of readers and to provide rich quantitative detail. This book by Edward R. Tufte provides examples of the most interesting and honest graphic work spanning the last 250 years. He describes how to make complex charts aesthetically pleasing to readers and the proper use of colors, proportions, and scaling. Tufte also compares and contrasts the effectiveness in conveying quantitative information through sentences, tables, and graphics. It includes 250 illustrations and is a valuable reference for authors seeking to communicate their quantitative findings in a truthful and interesting way to readers through the synergistic use of words, pictures, and numbers. (Two additional books have been printed after this one—all three are worth looking at.)

Van Wagenen, R. K. (1991). *Writing a thesis: Substance and style.* Englewood Cliffs, NJ: Prentice Hall.

This book is especially useful for graduate students who are just beginning to write or for scholars who lack organization, structure, or discipline in their writing. Van Wagenen provides a coherent structure for composing research documents and then provides detailed instructions about how to complete that structure. He provides tips throughout the book on how writing can be more forceful and effective. The book focuses on discussing the appropriate content for the introduction, methodology, results, and discussion sections of most academic papers. It provides advice on how important findings can be highlighted and how statistical results can be presented, and provides practical and pragmatic advice to writers throughout the scholarly writing process.

Witzling, L. P., & Greenstreet, R. C. (1989). *Presenting statistics: A manager's guide to the persuasive use of statistics.* New York: John Wiley.

This book focuses on how statistical information can be organized and presented to managerial decision makers. The book requires only a basic level of mathematical sophistication and provides step-by-step instructions on how to make persuasive presentations of statistical data. The book also makes suggestions on how to decide what quantitative information should be included in presentations. The authors provide more than 200 illustrations to make their points and focus on techniques that are available in most computer software applications.

Zinsser, W. (1991). *On writing well.* New York: HarperCollins. (Also available on Harper Audio.)

When you need a pep talk about the craft of writing, this book (or better yet the author's audiotape) will inspire and energize you. Many of the points made can be found in other places, but many are unique both in concept and in presentation. All evolve from the commonsense approach that author and reader have a relationship, and it is the writer's task to actively engage the reader through his or her personality. I found Zinsser's passion for editing especially helpful. He stresses the importance of well-chosen words and a conversational tone to convey even technical information (Connie Luoto).

Note

1. A few comments have been supplied by other authors, as indicated.

❧❀❧

About the Author

Anne Sigismund Huff is Professor of Strategic Management at the University of Colorado, Boulder, with a joint appointment at Cranfield School of Management in the United Kingdom. She received her PhD from Northwestern University and has been on the faculty at the University of California, Los Angeles, and the University of Illinois. Her research interests focus on strategic change, both as a dynamic process of interaction among firms and as a cognitive process affected by the interaction of individuals over time. She is the strategy editor for *Foundations in Organizational Science* and on the editorial board of the *Strategic Management Journal*, the *Journal of Management Studies*, and the *British Journal of Management*. In the 1998-1999 academic year, she is President of the Academy of Management.